Journey To A Dream

by Mary T. Lovel

Dedication

This book is dedicated to my sister,
Kathy Jensen, without whose
invaluable help I would still be
floundering around unpublished.

Copyright © 2006 by Mary T. Lovel
All rights reserved

ISBN# 978-1-4116-9145-2
First Edition
Printed in the USA

Published by Sherman Publishing, Sherman, Alaska
Cover art original oil painting by Mary T. Lovel
Editor and cover design by Kathy R. Jensen

Acknowledgements

My thanks to all my family for their contributions to this story and for
their encouragement and love.

TABLE OF CONTENTS

The Journey

Chapter 1   The Journey Begins

How well I remember all those years ago, the feelings I had of anticipation, fear of the unknown, even dread, laced with excitement about the adventure we were about to undertake. I couldn't sleep even though I was exhausted by all the work and preparation; getting everything ready, packing, sorting, selling all we could. We were actually leaving Missouri, moving to Alaska! Were we really going, at last?

Our four children were asleep, as was my husband Clyde. He had worked hardest of us all. He had built a camper shell of plywood for the back of our truck with a door on the back...the only window was on the door. He bolted an old car seat to the floor, and baby Lisa's portable crib also fit in there, leaving a small play area for our other three kids.

There were so many details; I can remember my head swimming with all the lists of things we thought we would need for our journey, wondering until the very early hours of morning if we would make it or not. What would we find when we got there? So many questions, the night filled with doubts; finally, toward morning, I slept.

Our oldest daughter Shelley was only eight when we started our trip on May 13, 1963. Our son Bud was six and a half, daughter Debbie five, and the baby Lisa was only ten and a half months old. They were eager and fresh from a good night's sleep, ready to go that morning. After saying good-byes all around, we all piled in, got comfortable, and Clyde started the truck. Attached to the back was our 41-foot house trailer, with all our worldly possessions packed inside. After about four feet the trailer wheels sunk down in a soft part of the driveway and we were stuck! What a beginning!

All of Clyde's family was there to see us off, and it was a good thing. They all helped dig us out, jack up the trailer, beef up the roadbed, and it all took time. The next thing I remember well, was riding down the long driveway almost to the highway, and getting the trailer stuck between two trees. Clyde's brother Glenn got us out with only a scratch on the trailer. Glenn drove big tractor-trailer trucks for years, and knew what he was doing. Clyde was learning fast; however, I never mastered the double clutch system on the truck, so Clyde had to drive all the way.

That first night and every night of the trip I can remember being sore all over from bumping around in the back of the truck. The kids were all really good, loving every minute of the adventure. They never got tired of riding because we stopped so very often; it seemed like we did more stopping and re-arranging or fixing, than riding. The first day we only made 125 miles altogether. I was sure it would be winter before we got there, at that rate.

It was tricky for Clyde, learning to pull something as big and cumbersome as the house trailer, with our 1949 ford three-quarter ton flatbed truck. The swaying was terrific at first, and the truck overheated quite badly, forcing us to stop often to cool it down. After the first few hills and curves, though, Clyde got the hang of it and handled it just fine.

We had enough groceries packed in boxes under the beds in the trailer to last us for about six weeks. Nothing perishable, all canned and instant foods. I fixed all our meals the whole trip, which probably didn't take any longer than eating out would have, but it felt like it at the time. It certainly was cheaper.

When we reached Nebraska, we had to buy a permit for $5.00 to drive through that state because we were 'over length and weight'. I remember that the roads weren't any too good, with no shoulders to pull a trailer over onto for stopping for meals or anything. We had to drive on to Beatrice, Nebraska to park for the night; the permit did not allow travel after dark. A few miles out of town we found a pipe and joint factory and parked in their parking lot. While we slept a terrible storm blew up, like a cyclone, complete with hail and strong winds. It blew out the picture window in the living room of the trailer and rain rushed in, soaking the living room and kitchen with torrents of water. The wind was so bad it actually lifted the trailer into the air and slammed it back down again several times. The kids slept through it all. As soon as the worst of the storm passed, Clyde and I mopped up the water and cleaned up the broken glass. We blocked the broken window with a piece of cardboard, then went back to bed to try to get a little sleep. The storm raged on for four hours. The next day we drove back to Beatrice, and had the window fixed.

It took us five days to get through Missouri and Nebraska to a small town called Bayard, Nebraska where we found ourselves on the first Friday since we left on our trip. It was evening, getting dark, and we were stuck for the weekend because of being over length and overweight for that state, we were not allowed to run after dark or on weekends. The reason I remember this town so well is because the town cop's name was Homer Lovell, no relation, but a coincidence just the same. He tried to get permission for us to go the few miles to the border with escort, so we could continue our trip the next day, to no avail. So we spent the weekend being stared at by all the townsfolk. We were parked in a bean and fertilizer plant lot next to the train depot, where the whole town drove down to park, got out of their cars, and stared at us. We spent the weekend doing laundry, visiting with the friendly folk of Bayard, and getting ready to start at first light Monday.

Our first flat tire (the first of many) happened 14 miles south of Buffalo, Wyoming a few days later. It was a puncture, and since we were going uphill at the time, we had no trouble. Fortunately we had all the necessary tools (including a gas powered air compressor) to fix our own flats, especially since all the flats seemed to occur miles from a service station.

The overheating problem kept up, though, and just before we got to Canada we had to have the radiator boiled out. We had had increasing problems with it boiling over, each day getting worse. The boiling out seemed to fix the problem, though. While we waited for the repairs to be finished we all took hot showers in the motel next door to the gas station, and how good they felt! After days of only sketchy pan baths, a hot shower was the height of luxury and for only $2 for the whole family. At least we entered Canada clean.

Chapter 2   Canada

T he roads were all better in Canada and there were roadside campsites or parks every 20 to 50 miles, so anyone could park there instead of just pulling over onto the shoulder of the road to eat and sleep. All the parks had water, toilets, tables and an enclosed kitchen so people could get out of the weather. These were completely equipped with wood cook stoves, wood to cook with, and tables inside. The people were all very friendly, and if we were stopped somewhere to fix a tire, or just to fix a meal, someone would always stop and ask us if we needed any help. It gave us a sense of security, knowing that if we really needed help, it would not be far off.

The cities were modern, but there were no mailboxes anywhere! We had saved up post cards and letters to our families, and tried to find a mailbox to send them off. No one even knew what a mailbox was! Finally we found a post office in a little general store, and of course we had to buy Canadian postage to put on our mail. We forgot we were foreigners!

The weather was nice and cool, cold at night, and didn't get dark until 10 pm; sunrise was about 3:30 am. The farther north we got, the longer daylight we had. By the time we got to Alaska, it wouldn't get dark at all. It was hard to imagine, night without darkness.

We met two families coming back from Fairbanks, heading for Texas. They were Air Force people. They told us there had been flooding to the east of Anchorage and a whole town, of about 1000 people had been evacuated, and the Alcan Highway was pretty muddy so we might have to stop and wait for it to dry out if it was very bad by the time we got there. We never found out which town those folks were talking about.

I also noticed the price of food, milk, bread, and especially produce was getting higher the farther north we got, and the price of gasoline, as well.

We developed a regular routine for fixing flats, as we had so many - and became quite good at it too. Shelley or Bud and I would jump on the flat tire to break it away from the rim. Clyde then took a big pry bar, pried the rubber up enough to remove the tube, and pumped it full of air with the air compressor. Next step was to wet the tube with a soap solution to find the leak, mark it, dry it off, let the air out again and glue a patch on the hole. When the patch was dry and set, he put the tube back in the tire, pumped it full of air again and we had a good tire once more. We became so adept that the entire procedure took only 20 minutes.

Looking back through our old travel journals refreshes my memory. We did enjoy our trip through Canada, averaging about 230 miles per day, and seven and a half to eight miles to the gallon! There were good places to camp every night with all the conveniences we liked, places for the kids to run and play. They enjoyed it all. Shelley and Bud would take turns riding up front with Clyde, but Debbie preferred to stay in back with me and baby Lisa. There she would color, snack, play with her doll or just look out the window. Then we got to Dawson Creek, BC.

Dawson Creek was a quaint rustic little town with a very definite 'frontier' feeling about it. There seemed to be an air of excitement and expectancy, perhaps of adventure about it. Probably that was just our feelings about finally having arrived at that point on our trip. The people all seemed happy, energetic, and enthusiastic about life in general. We thought it might have been the crystal clear air. It was wonderful. That was our 15th day on the road. The Alaska-Canadian Highway started there (name shortened to the Alcan Highway), 1250 miles of gravel road.

At the beginning of our trip, it very quickly became obvious that we needed some means of communication from the back of the truck to the front, since the truck lacked an access window or any other means of signaling to Clyde to stop so Clyde installed a set of field phones. I would whistle or yell loudly into my phone, and he would hear it on his phone, which was right near his head in the cab of the truck. Then all he had to do was pick up his phone, push the button and talk to me. It worked out quite well, especially when we were feeling the bumps too much in the back end of the truck, and needed to stop to stretch our legs. We only made 35 miles on that gravel road before we had to stop for the night. I wondered then how we would ever stand over 1200 miles more of it - just those few miles made us all sore and stiff with the jolting and jouncing. It was awful.

The truck began running badly, the dust and flying gravel were a plague - dust got into the trailer, and into our bedding, clothing, food, and water, everywhere. We couldn't figure out how dust got into the trailer in the first place, since we had sealed up every window and door, covered the vent pipes on the roof and any possible hole, to keep it out. If it weren't for the wonderful scenery around every bend, the trip would have been utterly miserable from that point on. But we parked in exotic sounding places like 'Prophet River', 'Peace River Bridge', places with the most gorgeous breathtaking scenery imaginable. We needed places like that to soothe our tired and battered bodies as we feasted our gritty watering eyes on the beauty everywhere.

In the middle of Fort Nelson, BC, our truck broke down, just quit right in the middle of the street and refused to run another inch. We had it towed to a station where they could work on it. It had taken us all day to go about 50 miles; the poor old truck just couldn't take it anymore. It took two days to get the burned out valve fixed and meanwhile we discovered that one of the rims on the trailer was bent, probably by an extra large boulder or a chuckhole somewhere between Dawson Creek and Fort Nelson. We had to buy another rim, which used up most of the rest of our money. We wired Clyde's mom back in Missouri, to send us some money to cover the rest of the trip.

Finally we were on our merry way once more, jouncing and bouncing up the road towards Alaska. We slept in gritty beds, ate gritty food and were generally miserable with all the dust and grime in the trailer. No matter how much we cleaned and washed clothes, the Alcan dust still lingered on, each day getting worse until one day, quite by accident, Clyde found where the dust was getting in. The cold air intake for the furnace, of all places! Neither of us had thought of that. After blocking and sealing off that hole, we took on no more dust; unfortunately the damage was already done. The rest of the trip on the gravel road was just as eventful. It was slow, tiring, and beautiful. We also had some pretty close calls, nearly losing it all.

After parking by a pretty little river to have lunch one sunny and beautiful day, as we packed up and were ready to leave Clyde started the truck, inched forward slowly and the trailer promptly sank down to its axles on the right, tilting dangerously and hanging over the river. We all jumped out of the truck and stood looking at it and wondering what to do next. It was a fearsome sight. All of our worldly possessions were in that trailer, and if it went over into the river, we would have nothing left at all. The rapidly running river was about 25 feet down a steep bank, which looked like the trailer would just tip and fall right in. Clyde tried to use a jack, but the ground was too soft. Finally someone came by and offered to stop at the next place to call for a tow truck to pull us out. After about an hour, the tow truck came, hooked on to the front of our truck, and he promptly got stuck. While the men were trying to figure out what to do next, a wonderful big semi came along headed towards us. The driver stopped, looked the situation over, hooked the front of his semi on to the front of the tow truck, still hooked to our truck and trailer, and backed up. Just like that, all of us came unstuck. It took the power of that large truck to do it though, and whenever we see a Lynden Transfer truck to this day, we think of that nice man with thanks. He didn't even stay around long enough for us to get his name. We certainly met a lot of people that day.

After that adventure, it was good to get to Liard Hot Springs and bathe in that wonderful hot water. There was a nice little pool with bathhouses to change in, about a quarter of a mile off the road. We parked the truck and trailer on the side of the road and walked in. No one else was there, so we had the place all to ourselves. Someone told us later on down the road that the water stays at 116 degrees at the hottest part of the pools even when the temperature is 40 degrees below zero in the winter and there is lots of snow on the ground. We all felt so clean, and rested all night very well indeed. I would have liked to stay right there for a week, at least. It was the cleanest we had felt since hitting the gravel road; that was our fifth night on the Alcan.

Later the next day the back door on the trailer came open, sucking in another trailer load of dust and grit. We had to tape it closed because the bumping had shaken the lock loose and it wouldn't latch anymore. So all our cleaning went for nothing.

Every time we stopped for anything at all, the kids would jump out and run, pick up some gravel and come running back to ask us if there was gold in it. They sure had a good time on that trip.

Before we left Missouri, Clyde installed electric brakes on the trailer, since the trailer weighed a lot more than the truck, and the truck's brakes weren't powerful enough to stop both truck and trailer. However, on the gravel road flying rocks and such repeatedly cut the trailer brake lines, so every time we came to a hill, he would test the trailer brakes to see if they still worked. The first time he discovered no brakes on the trailer almost ended our trip, a heart-stopping event, to be sure. It was a long, steep downhill grade with a sharp drop off on both sides. I could feel the truck picking up speed, and see the trailer skittering sideways, or trying to pass the truck, at least it looked that way from my vantage point. I grabbed the field phone, thinking that Clyde had fallen asleep at the wheel, and yelled as loud as I could, but there was no answer and we seemed to be going even faster. It was one of the times when all the kids were in back with me, napping. It was an awful feeling, not knowing if Clyde was awake, or in control, or what was happening. I could see the terrible chasms on either side of the road; the trailer was swaying sickeningly back and forth across the entire road, and I thought we were all going to die right there. Finally I felt the speed slowing a little, and then a little more, until at last we came to a stop. I had kept yelling into the phone, but Clyde never answered.

After about five minutes, he came back and asked, "Are you all okay?" as he opened the camper door. He was white as a sheet. After finding out we were all okay, he got out the electrician's tape and wire strippers, explaining what happened and why he didn't answer the phone. "I couldn't let go of the steering wheel, it was all I could do to hold the truck on the road, the brakes didn't work on the trailer and I had to keep going faster to keep ahead of the trailer." He went on to explain that the truck brakes wouldn't slow the trailer down at all and by the time we were at the bottom of the hill, he was going 90 miles per hour! He let the momentum take us up to the top of the next hill, and then stopped. Luckily no one was coming from the other direction. By the time he finished explaining, he had stopped shaking, especially knowing we were all okay. He fixed the brake lines, but there was no way to get the lines out of the path of flying gravel; after that, he fixed the lines before going down a hill.

Every time we stopped, there was a vista more magnificent than the last time until we got to the point where we knew we'd seen the best there ever could be, but the next view was even better, somehow, taking nothing away from the previous scenes.

Chapter 3 North to Alaska

When we entered Yukon Territory, we realized rapidly that the road was even worse. We had two flat tires in a short time. It was like driving on a gigantic washboard, with ruts all over, and potholes in between. We parked that night at Morley River, tired, tired. Even the kids seemed tired that night and we all hoped that was the worst of it, and prayed for better road conditions. But the next day the road was even worse (if that's possible) and we had three blowouts with completely ruined tires. It was a good thing we had extras all around. We parked in Mendenhall Campground that night, and we all slept in the campground kitchen, because Clyde got the trailer stuck, firmly, between two trees, hung up on the back end on high gravel, tilted at such an angle that we would all fall out of bed if we tried sleeping in it. The man who looked after the campground and ran the grocery store gave us permission to sleep in the campground kitchen, and use the wood stove in there for heat. We set up Lisa's crib and the rest of us slept on the tables. The next morning the man from the store came with his three-ton truck and pulled the trailer out. It took quite a bit of time and work digging, jacking and shifting to get the trailer out; the man hooked his truck to the trailer and pulled it all the way out, and onto the highway where Clyde again hooked our truck to it, and after much thanks, we went on our way. We didn't want that to happen again.

Thankfully the road wasn't as bad as it had been, and people we talked to along the way all said it was good all the way to the Alaska border, but that the paved road, which starts in Alaska, was terrible. We really didn't want to hear that. That was at Milepost 968, our eighth night on the Alcan. It felt like that road would never end.

The next night we camped at Kluane Lake, but not in the campground, since it looked like the one we got stuck in, and Clyde did not want to take a chance getting stuck again.

After we got the kids settled down for the night, Clyde and I took a walk, but before we went far, a man from the highway department stopped to ask us if we were having trouble. We assured him we were fine, and explained why we had not pulled into the campground. He agreed that the roads into and out of the campground were too narrow for an outfit such as ours. After a nice visit he left, and we slowly sauntered on. It was still light out, but sort of dusky, when we heard eerie wild laughter, like some demented creature from a horror movie. It made goose bumps pop out all over. We didn't see anything, but the insane laughter seemed to come from the water. We decided to cut our stroll short and go to bed. We locked the doors, feeling very foolish when Clyde remembered, from a Jack London story he read years ago, that those awful noises had to come from a loon. We asked a park ranger the next day if there were loons around, and he laughed and said, "You must have heard one laughing, eh? Scares everyone first time hearing one."

Chapter 4   Alaska

On June 6th, 1963, at 8:10 pm Alaska time, we finally crossed the border into Alaska. That had been one busy day. At Burwash Flats Camp, still in Canada, we stopped to help an old man who had run off the road, stranding his truck on top of a mound of dirt. A forest ranger came along shortly after we stopped and we all pitched in and dug for a couple of hours; then Clyde put the snatch block on the uphill side of the old man's one ton truck and hooked it to our truck for stability, so it wouldn't tip over, and the ranger drove it out. The old man was from Arkansas and had fallen asleep at the wheel, ran off the road into the ditch and up onto the mound of dirt before he woke up. So we had to not only dig it out, but also build a road under his truck to keep it from falling into the chasm on the other side. He was a very nice man, just tired from driving too long. After the old man was out of his predicament, we went on our way, and the road was fairly good, but the terrible, interminable dust went on and on and we knew we would never feel clean again. We had to drive with our headlights on at all times because the thick cloud of dust hanging in the air made visibility very poor. But as soon as we hit the border, everything changed. No longer did the road seem to go by with a muted roar, it was so quiet we wondered if the engine was running. After 1250 miles of gravel and holes, pits, and ruts, it was wonderful - for about 100 yards – then we hit a frost heave and thought we had broken everything, including our bones. It couldn't be seen until the truck was right on top of it, and then it was too late. We stopped, of course and Clyde inspected everything, while I saw to the kids to see what damage was done. Poor little Debbie bit her tongue, Bud bumped his head, Shelley fell off the seat and bruised her leg and baby Lisa sat down hard, scaring herself, they were all crying; we soothed them into good spirits once again and were on our way for a few miles. It was slower than ever though. Some dishes were broken and a large mirror in the bathroom of the trailer, but otherwise, except for things being tossed around, it seemed that the damage was light.

The constant daylight fooled us - it seemed like it should get dark sometime, but it never did; just dusky about midnight to 1:30 am, then the sun was way up there again and stayed up in the sky longer than we'd ever seen. Unreal as it seemed, we felt we had more pep and energy; whether imagination or reality, it was great because we had put in many long days of driving, sometimes until 11 pm before realizing it was way past time to quit, and we'd wake up ready to go again around 5 am.

I was certainly not crazy about my first look at Alaska; after the magnificent scenery we had been through for days on end, here we were at this place which seemed flat, with stunted trees, and not much to look at except a lot of the same thing - quite a letdown. The frost heaves in the road and the broken pavement and potholes were worse than the gravel road had been by far, and slower driving, too. The only good thing about it was, no dust! Blessed relief.

The mosquitoes were ferocious, and totally famished. We presented fresh blood from afar, and they all took advantage of it. Much of the land we traveled through at that point was swampy, a veritable paradise for mosquitoes.

Four miles into Alaska, the fan belt broke on the truck, and the only ones Clyde had in the box of spare parts were too small. We limped along to a place called Seaton's Café, hoping they might have a fan belt to fit. Our first night in Alaska, at last! But in the morning, much to our dismay, we found out that they didn't have a fan belt, so Clyde hitchhiked nine miles to the next place and got one, but it was the wrong size, and the only one they had besides. The only thing to do was to jury-rig one out of a piece of rubber, and he unhooked the truck from the trailer and taking Bud with him, left the girls and I with the trailer fixing lunch while waiting. He only got three miles before the jury-rigged belt broke, but then a man came along and stopped to ask if he could help. It so happened he had a fan belt of the perfect size, and just gave it to Clyde saving him a 29 mile round trip to the last place we had passed. So we continued on jolting, bucking and jumping our way to Tok, 40 miles before we got to Tok we broke a spring on the trailer, and some nice folks from Texas helped us limp in on three springs. Clyde had it welded together and blocked, because the only other alternative was to wait a week or ten days there for one to be shipped in from Seattle or Anchorage, if anyone would have one there, and it was doubtful. The spring didn't break in half, but a couple of the leaves broke on it, and another bump or two it would have broken all the way, maybe turning us over.

We only had 314 miles to go at that point, and I had my doubts from time to time if we would make it the rest of the way. Up to that point, we had sustained eleven flat tires, three complete blowouts, broken fan belt, burned out valve, cut the trailer brake lines in half five or six times, gotten stuck several times having to be towed or pulled out, and nearly lost it all at least twice. God surely does watch out for fools and little children. We continued slowly and carefully on our way.

After traveling on the Glenn Highway for a while, we discovered that the scenery was greatly improved. The mountains were magnificent; all the way down they got better and better until it seemed that Alaska was made out of layer upon layer of mountains. Such grandeur and breathtaking beauty is beyond description. The mountains surrounding Anchorage, called the Chugach Range, were wonderful - what a view to behold. We could see them from all the windows of our trailer.

Chapter 5   Our First Alaska Home

O n June 10th, 1963 at 9 pm, we finally arrived in Anchorage, at long last. We were too tired to do anything but park for the night, and in the morning we found a nice trailer park to set up the trailer in. We spent the entire day leveling and blocking up the trailer, meeting our neighbors, and keeping track of the kids.

Clyde, Bud and Lisa Lovel at Spenard Acres Trailer Court

Thank goodness we had food left, enough for about two weeks. We only had about $2.75 left, and were hoping that Clyde's last paycheck was there in General Delivery at the Post Office. We called both sets of parents and found out that none of the postcards and letters we had mailed in Canada had arrived; they were beginning to worry and so were relieved to find out we had arrived safely.

Our neighbors across the road come over and invited us all to come over to dinner for fresh salmon, which we had never tasted before. We were in the yard at the time, beating the dust and grit out of our mattresses. That was a friendly and neighborly thing to do, and we really appreciated the invitation, and better yet, the dinner, which consisted of mounds of crispy fried red salmon, mashed potatoes, fresh hot cornbread, and a big salad. Was that ever scrumptious! We certainly made a dent in all that food. Our kids ate like they hadn't eaten all month, and still there was food left over. What a great cook Frances was. Mac, her nice husband, and cute kids too, all promptly made friends with our kids and us. A good start for our new life, just beginning; all of us healthy, the truck still ran, our house still all in one piece, (more or less,) even though I despaired of ever getting it clean again.

We wondered how we would like living in a trailer park, since we had never lived in one - in Missouri our trailer was parked on a lot, surrounded on two sides with trees, and was relatively private, at the end of a road near Clyde's mom's house. We knew this would take some getting used to, but we also knew it would not be for long, since we planned to start looking for land to homestead as soon as possible. Looking out our windows, we could look right into a neighbor's window, and it sort of felt like living in a fish bowl.

Once we had things more or less organized, we discovered our little Debbie was shoeless. When we started from St. Louis she had three pairs of shoes and a pair of slippers. She hated shoes for some reason, and took every opportunity to take them off. She managed to lose at least one shoe of each pair somewhere along the way, and hunt though we would, we never could find her lost shoes. One left shoe and her pair of slippers was all there were left. Bud managed to lose a couple of tee shirts, and Shelley lost one of my good mixing spoons, probably digging in the dirt somewhere along the way, a favorite pastime for all the kids.

All things taken into consideration, we didn't do too badly for 28 days of travel with four small kids. We had time along the way to enjoy lots of beauty, met many nice people, learned a lot about many things, and had quite an adventure. We certainly had never done anything remotely like that before. The total trip was about 4900 miles, the longest trip we had ever taken. I admire my wonderful husband, doing all the driving with no one to relieve him, and actually getting us safely to Alaska, all the way from Missouri. That had to be some tremendous accomplishment, no matter how you look at it. I couldn't imagine then why I had resisted going for nine years!

How did the pioneers in covered wagons EVER do it with no roads at all, only wagon rut trails? They would have thought our 1250-mile gravel road a superhighway!

Chapter 6   The Interim

For the next 15 months we lived in Anchorage in our little trailer-home, and learned many things about our new home state. There were many friendly people in our trailer court, and all of them full of information about our new home. We also learned much about fishing, canning, winter, and living in 24 hour daylight conditions, to name a few.

The day after we arrived we went to the post office and found, to our delight and relief, that Clyde's paycheck was there. We used part of it to turn on the electricity, and pay the space rent in the trailer park, bought some groceries and a fishing license for Clyde. He liked to fish more than I did.

We were certainly glad we had brought our little home with us, as we thought rents were outlandish. To get one unfurnished room it was $150 a month with or without a private bath! Our space rent was $40 a month, with water included. The trailer park was provided with water from an artesian well, the sweetest and coldest (always at 34 degrees) water we had ever tasted. The air was invigorating and fresh, and the kids continued to thrive, and eat like horses. Even though Clyde and I were still tired after two days, the fresh air made us feel alive and energetic, also it was wonderful for sound sleep.

The city of Anchorage was certainly on the ball, as we were only there for two days before the personal property taxman came around to give us a form to fill out on all our personal property! Our trailer, as it stood, was worth more than we had paid for it brand new, and even if it did slow us down considerably, we were doubly glad we had brought it along.

In June we had about 20 hours of bright sunshine, and the other four hours were just dusk, when the sun disappeared behind a mountain for a rest. We could read a newspaper outside at midnight, if we were so inclined. Eventually we thought we might get used to it, but the kids kept resisting going to bed each night, exclaiming, "But mommy, it's still daytime!" I knew immediately I would have to put heavier curtains on their bedroom windows. Clyde and I were usually tired enough each night to go to bed at the usual time even if it was broad daylight. The temperature in the day was around 64 degrees.

We found Alaska to be a unique place, with ever changing weather; sometimes it would rain for an hour or so and then it would be cloudy for the rest of the day, with intermittent sunshine coming through, or it would be sunny all day, never getting hot and muggy as we were used to in Missouri, but always with a cool breeze. Sometimes it would only rain at night, or when it was supposed to be night, though when it was raining or with heavy clouds, the light would be dimmer, at least.

A big event at that time was when a ship would come in to the Port of Anchorage. This was even televised live and usually there was no TV during the day at all - it came on about 6 PM, both stations. The ferry Malasphina came in to port the first Saturday we were there; this was a passenger ship smaller than the Admiral in St. Louis. The ferry took passengers to Homer and other places where there were no roads connecting to other towns. The radio stations reported news of the ship's impending arrival three days before the ship got into port, having kept in touch by ship-to-shore radio. It really seemed funny, after living in San Diego and St. Louis where boats were just routine. I guessed not many large ships came in because when the tide was out, Cook Inlet was about half mud flats. The tide never went out or came in at the same time each day, but you could stand by the Inlet and see it come in huge waves. Anchorage has the second highest and lowest tides in the world; the tides come in fast, and begin to go out again just as fast, about 12 hours later. We were told that people had lost their lives while stranded on the mud flats when the tide comes in.

Our first excursion out of town was to Portage Glacier, toward Seward, on the Seward Highway, about 50 miles south of Anchorage; the scenery was wonderful. The glacier was just a huge field of old ice between two mountains with a small lake at the base of it, separating the glacier from the parking lot. Though it was approximately one-third to one-fourth mile across the little lake to the actual glacier, the cold emanating from the ice was clearly felt. The brilliant turquoise blue colors in the ice were amazing, and some of the chunks of ice, which had broken off the glacier and were floating in the water, were as large as buildings. When a chunk broke off, (it was called 'calving') we could hear it clearly. There are glaciers all over the state; only the largest ones have names. Today, Portage Glacier has receded so far back between the mountains it cannot be seen from shore and the lake is huge. The glacier itself has receded some five miles back. One can hike to the glacier on trails around the lake or take the excursion boat right up to the glacier itself, but it can't be seen except in glimpses through a powerful telescope located in the new visitors center/observation building located there now. There is also a nice restaurant located near the parking lot. But in 1963 there was nothing there but a place to park and the huge glistening awesome glacier.

People told us that the salmon were beginning to run heavily in some of the streams, south of Anchorage, and so at the first opportunity Clyde went fishing with some of the men from the trailer court, and came home with two big red salmon. Were they ever good! They told us that when the salmon were running heavily, you didn't even need a fishing pole or a line, just a net, and you could take your pick. They said the streams got so full that you couldn't wade in them for the fish. The salmon came from the ocean and swam upstream in the creeks and rivers to spawn, and then they died. You had to catch them before they got to the spawning grounds. The men also told Clyde that when you got tired netting the fish, you just snagged them. It sounded to me like you could get all the fish you would ever want to eat in a very short time.

We found out that the wild berries all got ripe about August, and that there were cranberries, raspberries, strawberries, and blueberries, among others. I was amazed to see that dandelions grew there too - everything else seemed so different.

On one of the peaks of the Chugach Mountains we could see from our trailer was the NIKE Missile site, which was, we were told, our protection from Russia. It was a deterrent in the Cold War. Way up there at the missile site there were winds which blew almost constantly in winter, from 100 and 110 miles per hour, but not much wind below in the city

Food prices were rather high compared to what we had been used to in Missouri, but we found if we watched the ads in the newspaper we could take advantage of the sales on whatever was advertised and come out almost as well. I baked all our bread and saved money there, since flour was nearly always on sale at one store or the other. Switching to concentrated milk saved money as well. This was not condensed milk, but concentrated whole milk, which tasted just like regular milk when you added water to it. It came in plastic bags. I had never seen it sold anywhere until we came to Alaska. I thought it was a great idea and a space saver for refrigerators too. Freight charges were what made prices so high here - everything had to be shipped in and it was such a long way from the States. (The Lower 48)

There were so many new things to do here, - salmon fishing, getting clothes and shoes for school, finding out about school for the kids. Fortunately, the elementary school was only about four blocks away from the trailer park. Some of the kids in the trailer park told Shelley about ice skating on the playground and other winter sports the schools fixed up for the children. In the winter, when the temperature got cold enough, they flooded the playgrounds with water and made ice rinks for all the kids to skate on.

In 1963 there were 92,000 people living in the entire Anchorage area, including Spenard, Mountain View, Turnagain and all the other areas in a ten-mile radius. Anchorage was also noted for the second highest tides in the world, with 35 - 40 foot high tides. It was known as the most air minded city in the world, with one out of every 55 Alaskans holding a pilot's license. Over 400,000 passengers passed through Anchorage International Airport in 1962. The growing season in the Greater Anchorage area was approximately 100 days. The longest day of the year - June 21 - the summer solstice, at 19 ½ hours of daylight and the shortest day, December 21, at 5 hours and 29 minutes. Record high temperature as of 1963 was 86 degrees and record low was minus 38 degrees. Alaska has NO SNAKES!!

Clyde took Bud with him to Bird Creek fishing, and they came back with nine beautiful pink salmon. Mac came over to look at them and told Clyde that the limit was three fish in possession per person per day. We were fortunate the game warden wasn't nearby, as the fines were stiff, $100. - $500. We had thought there was no limit on pink or red salmon, only on king salmon. Clyde obtained a fishing regulation brochure and sure enough, there it was, in fine print. They were all over 16 inches long too, and our freezer was stuffed full of fish, no room even for ice cubes. I knew I'd have to start canning fish soon. It was a good thing we all liked eating fish since we had so much; we had been eating fish every day. I found many ways to prepare salmon, and found it was really tasty.

We planted a little garden at the back of the yard, and fenced it in to keep kids and moose out. We planted spinach, carrots, turnips, radishes and lettuce. It was late for planting, but we were told that they would grow, and be ready to eat in four to five weeks.

We continued to have trouble getting the kids to go to bed in the daylight. They really carried on about it, heartily objecting, and just not settling down to sleep. I had trouble keeping track of the time myself. We would be working out in the yard, the kids playing and being good, and all of a sudden it would be 10 pm before we knew it. Of course the kids would get tickled whenever they could stay up late, and it would all be "Mom's fault."

On July 20th 1963 we witnessed an almost total (96%) eclipse of the sun. It certainly was weird and strange. It got very dark and the temperature suddenly dropped by 10 degrees. We could look at the sun directly, through exposed film negatives, without harming our eyes.

My mom sent me a can sealer so that I could can all the salmon we were catching and free up the freezer for meat when the time came. It worked very well and I spent several days canning fish and labeling them and storing them in boxes under the beds. By this time we were getting rather tired of fish, though with no money coming in, at least it was food.

Some of our neighbors gave us some caribou burger, and a roast. A welcome change from salmon all the time. It was delicious, somewhat like venison, only better. We looked forward to hunting season.

Meanwhile, I kept busy sewing warm things for winter, for all the kids, and doing some ironing for a lady in the trailer park, for a little money to keep milk and other odds and ends on the table. We had both been applying for jobs as one of us had to work. Clyde was going out daily on interviews, and several promising positions were to be available within a few weeks.

Our radishes were ready to eat, and the spinach and turnips would be ready in a week, and lettuce soon thereafter. We bought the heading kind by mistake, which takes longer than the leaf lettuce. But it had only been a little over three weeks since we planted the seeds, and we were amazed at how quickly everything grew, despite what we had been told and what we had read. To see it with your own eyes, day-by-day pushing up an inch or two was astounding.

At that time in the summer, about midway through, we had 18 hours of total daylight, about four hours of dusk, and almost two nearly dark hours. The days were getting shorter. The weather had been very nice so far, and everyone we talked to said that this was the slowest summer they had seen in years, construction wise, and otherwise. It seemed that when the construction season was off, or slow, every other type of job was scarce as well. We had met a lot of people, made many new friends, and really liked what we had seen so far of the country, so totally different than anything we had experienced. Everything would have been perfect if we only had an income. We were beginning to panic, since all our bills would be coming due soon.

The kids continued to be healthy, full of energy and pep, and Lisa was a little terror. She learned to climb up on all the furniture, and I couldn't keep her out of anything. She had a great tan from playing out in the yard so much, as did all the kids.

No one locked their trailers or cars then, the crime rate was so low. Our little Debbie, friendly child that she was, had been making herself at home here and there, unbeknownst to us of course, just walking in, sitting down, turning on the TV. We found out quite by accident when one of our neighbors came holding Debbie by the hand, and told us that he and his wife had just come back from the store and found Debbie calmly sitting on their couch, eating one of their apples, watching cartoons on TV. She just smiled and said, "Where have you been? I came to visit!" They thought we probably didn't know, and they were right! We thought she was playing in the yard behind the trailer where she often played, building things. After asking around, we discovered this was a regular pastime for Debbie; that she had a regular route, and "visited" a lot of friends whether they were home or not. No one but us seemed to mind, but we were very embarrassed. She did no damage, except to help herself to a cookie or an apple, which she was used to doing at her Grandma's house in Missouri. She had no idea it was wrong until we explained everything to her; we had to make other arrangements with the gate on the fence, so it wasn't so easy to open. Debbie had always had a "wandering foot", but eventually grew out of it.

Shelley, Bud, Debbie & Lisa Lovel swimming in icy water

Clyde went to work, finally, on the last day of July, 1963. It was only a temporary job with Civil Service, painting heavy equipment. He was told it might work into a permanent job. It was nice to be able to once more pay the bills.

We went berry picking near the end of August, and got both high and low bush cranberries, and saw many other people out picking too. I made 20 pints of jelly from what we picked, and it seemed like it took no time at all to pick so many berries. We would be picking wild blueberries and raspberries the following week, but I had seen an article in the paper about bear trouble they had in Fairbanks, because of the poor berry crop there. It had been so dry that the berries were all stunted and small, and three men had been attacked in separate incidents in as many weeks. One of them was killed. The berry crop near Anchorage seemed to me to be wonderful, probably because we had had more rain than Fairbanks. At least we hadn't seen any sign of bears. We decided to take the gun with us the next time we went berry picking.

Moose hunting season would be opening soon and Clyde was going hunting with a neighbor who had a swamp buggy, a machine equipped to go through all types of terrain. With a swamp buggy, you wouldn't have to pack the game out of the woods on your back. It would take quite a few trips to get one moose out, since they weigh from 900 - 1500 pounds.

Our garden continued to yield plenty, for so small a patch. We enjoyed fresh spinach, mustard, and turnip greens cooked together as well as salads of lettuce and large juicy radishes, the size of silver dollars. The turnips were disappointing - small, strong tasting, and mostly full of worms. We finally got to taste moose meat, and thought it delicious.

Lisa had her first birthday in June, and by the end of summer was talking a lot and chasing after the neighbors' puppy and trying to bark like it did. The weather had cooled a bit by August, and days were getting shorter.

It was time to go to the Alaska State Fair in Palmer, and we were all looking forward to it, since we hadn't been on any trips out of town for a while. We thought we would look over the area as well, and drive up to Wasilla, and Willow, if the weather was warm enough, and have a big picnic, do a little trout fishing, and just enjoy the weekend. Winter was coming on fast, and we hadn't been anywhere since we arrived in Anchorage except to Portage Glacier, Bird Creek, and Otter Lake, all within 25 miles or so of Anchorage. We thought the kids would get a big kick out of the fair too, and of course they loved picnics.

Late in August, we went to the State Fair in Palmer, located in the Matanuska Valley, a beautiful lush valley surrounded by gorgeous mountains, snow capped, and lovely. We were astounded at the size of the vegetables shown at the fair; there was an immense 65-pound cabbage, turnips the size of large honeydew melons or bigger, and radishes that made our silver dollar-sized ones look tiny. It was really something. We had heard about and read about the large vegetables grown here, but seeing them in person was simply amazing. There was a large building with farm animals in it, being shown and a horse show, horse races, and a parade. There were carnival type rides, a Ferris wheel, merry-go-round, pony rides, etc., a spook house and all kinds of booths. There was a 4-H project display that covered every kind of program the 4-H clubs had; and home-baked and canned goods and all sorts of things like that. I found everything interesting and different, never having been to a State Fair before; I had only been to the World's Fair when I was very small, and didn't remember any of it.

Clyde had never been to a State Fair before either, so it was all new and different and very educational for us. There was even a live reindeer there. The kids had a great time. We spent the entire day trying to take in everything. All types of stuffed animals were on display, from a mink clear up to a polar bear and even a buffalo. We found out there are buffalo in Alaska, too, along with everything else, although they aren't a species native to Alaska.

After we left the fair we drove up to Willow and parked by the Big Willow River, built a fire on the gravel bank, and cooked hamburgers and had our dinner. I brought along a potato salad and some tomatoes and all the usual picnic fixings. The whole day was beautiful and we were all tired when we finally got home, but we were really glad we went.

Debbie at the State Fair in Palmer

Bud and Shelley started school at Willowcrest Elementary, and liked it just fine. Unfortunately, Debbie was too young to start first grade, and they had no kindergarten, except for six weeks in the summer, and she was too young to go in the summer session as well. She was really disappointed.

Toward the end of September, the weather had cooled down somewhat, being in the high 50's, not quite getting up into the 60's anymore, and down to about 35 at night. It had rained, and the mountains all around were covered with snow, to about a third of the way down. It really put a nip in the air. Days were growing shorter by about six minutes a day

We found an old beat up Cadillac, which ran, and paid a hundred dollars for it, which enabled me to drive the kids to their various activities, and to the doctor for the required school physicals. At about the same time, a boy came around giving away puppies, and he had only one left, a female, about five weeks old, very cute, half toy poodle and half Scottie. She was black, and acted more like a cat than a dog. The kids were crazy about her, of course, and they named her "Hey Girl". They cleaned up after her and fed her and it gave them something to do on days when they had to stay in. She was a good puppy, already house broken, (a real plus), but I hadn't wanted to be bothered - it was Clyde, (old softie), who said we would take her when the boy who brought her to the door said he was going to take her out and shoot her if he couldn't find a home for her, his parents told him not to bring any of the pups home.

It wasn't until October 26th that we got our first snow. It had been very windy and chilly, lots of snow on the mountains and northern lights many nights in a row, very bright and colorful. The most amazing thing to watch. We got what the natives here called "snow flurries", which amounted to about five inches. That's what we considered a 'heavy' snowfall in Missouri. Of course the kids were all thrilled. Lisa and Hey Girl played in the snow and had a wonderful time

We all went to the National Guard Armory to a 'Hootenanny', which was lots of fun, with all local talent.

It really took a long time to get mail from the States to Alaska. We missed our families so much, and when we did get mail from them, it was like a celebration, a real treat.

We bought ice skates for the three older kids at the Salvation Army Thrift store for $1. per pair. The janitor had flooded the school playground and ice-skating had begun in earnest. The girls and Bud learned rapidly and loved skating.

In early November we had more snow, another seven inches fell on top of the first five inches. The temperature stayed at right around 20 degrees. Then we had a Chinook, which is a warm wind from the Japanese currents in the ocean that comes every once in a while throughout the winter. Our neighbor told us that even if it happens to be 40 degrees below zero when the Chinook comes, you just take off your coat or you would sweat so much you would freeze to death when the wind stops. It melts the snow and ice and when it stops blowing, it gets cold again almost instantly, as cold as it was before the Chinook, and everything freezes over again. It was really strange. We had almost a foot of snow on the ground, and then in a matter of a few days, nothing but water, and then when it stopped, ice all over the place.

The kids left for school every day with long underwear, leggings, sweaters, coats, mittens, wool socks, boots and caps, and it was dark when they left in the morning, just beginning to get light. Soon they would have to carry flashlights. We didn't have to worry about them walking, because there were at least a dozen other kids from the trailer park going to the school, and they all walked together. Also there were no busy streets to cross or woods to go through. They were on half-day sessions until the other school was finished in December, then they would go all day.

I learned to knit, and did a fair job of it too, having taken a few classes at the Knit Shop, which were free if you bought your supplies from them. I started on slippers, and then it was mittens and then it was sweaters, all made out of wonderful thick Canadian wool yarn. The sweaters were quite complicated, with designs and all, and lined and with zippers. I managed to get through two of them, and then called a halt.

November turned out to be a terrible month for everyone, not just Alaskans, our whole country was in mourning for our President Kennedy, assassinated. What a terrible blow. The same day Clyde was laid off his job.

In December, three days before Christmas, the landlord made us get rid of the puppy, setting forth a new rule they just made to make the trailer court pet-free. The kids were all devastated. We called the SPCA and they sent a man with two small boys over to get her, so she would have a good home and be loved.

We had a lean Christmas, but not too bad. Clyde made several toys for the kids, and I knitted them all new mittens. There was absolutely no snow on the ground at all, and it was 40 degrees. That Chinook we had lasted for nearly a week. The weather was 35 to 40 degrees all that time, and we nearly roasted. Then it rained a couple of times and after the rain it was cold again for two days, only 5 degrees, and ice was everywhere, sheets of it. Since then it hadn't been below twenty degrees, warming up during the short days to 35. Who would ever have believed there would be no snow for Christmas, in Alaska???

Clyde and Buddy drove out into the woods the day before Christmas and cut a little tree, while the girls and I stayed home and made decorations out of colored paper, glue and glitter, and the bottoms of egg cartons cut in sections and glued together. We couldn't find our lights, so we thought we had left them behind. It was a pretty little tree and very old fashioned.

The kids were out of school until January 6th, and then they would be on full day sessions, and have hot lunches too, for 35c a day. We had only 4 ½ hours of daylight but each day was gaining a bit, after December 21st, the shortest day of the year. All the school-age kids got flashlights for Christmas, as well.

On New Years Day it snowed all day long - seven inches worth of great big fluffy flakes. We went over to a friend's house on the Army base, and had New Years dinner with their family. We took their oldest child and ours to a movie on the base, "20,000 Leagues Under the Sea."

My Grandmother sent Shelley a real sealskin coat, and she loved it. It looked very nice on her and was very warm. Debbie and I both wished it fit us. So far it had been too warm for a fur coat, but no doubt that would change, and it did. It had been snowing off and on ever since the first day of the year and staying around 30 degrees most of the time.

A neighbor of ours in the trailer court, also good friends, moved back to the States and since they were flying back, they didn't take much with them. They gave us all their breakable dishes, glasses, and a ton of food, pillows, blankets, and all kinds of stuff, including two parakeets, a cage and food for them. One of the birds was green, and the other blue, and they were named Pete and Repeat. The kids were thrilled, of course. All the cupboards in the house were full of canned goods plus a couple of big boxes in the closet, which really helped out a lot. They also gave us about 50 pounds of prime moose steak, when they emptied their freezer. It all helped so much, since we were, at that time, living on unemployment insurance.

Sled dog races started, in preparation for the annual Fur Rendezvous, which was in February. We had never seen a live dog team and so we went to the races, and were thrilled by the excitement of it all. It was fun, and we looked forward to "Fur Rondy" as it was nicknamed, and still is.

It wasn't long before the temperature dropped to 10 degrees below zero, just after mid-January. That was the coldest it had been for two months or more. The truck wouldn't even start, and the car was frozen solid, it seemed. We had wrapped the pipes under the trailer with insulation and heat tapes, and insulated the skirting around the trailer, so none of the water or drains were frozen. Clyde did whatever he needed to do to get the vehicles running once more, and plugged them both in so hopefully that would not happen again. There was no bus service in those days, except way downtown, and we were miles from downtown then, in Spenard.

When Fur Rendezvous started, it was a big weeklong party, actually ten days in all, put on to break up the winter since it is so long. All the miners and trappers living out in the bush came into town to sell their furs and trade for whatever they needed. There were dog races, auctions, dances, and all sorts of arts and crafts, food booths, and a general feeling of fun. We attended as much as we could, and had a wonderful time. We saw Eskimo shows, and went to the fur auction, and attended all three days of the dog races. We really liked those races, they were exciting, and the dogs were so eager to run! They were tired at the end of the 25-mile race each day, but still willing to pull and run for all they were worth. They were beautiful. It was all so different from anything we had ever seen before. There were 27 teams in the races, and they all started in town from 4th Avenue in Anchorage and then out onto the trail and around a small lake and back into town for the finish - 25 miles a day for three days.

The Eskimo dances were different too, very enjoyable. They used walrus stomachs stretched over hoops as drums and most of the Eskimo people wore beautiful fur parkas and mukluks, which are a kind of fur boot they made themselves. What wonderful craftsmen they are!

Shelley and Bud were doing well in school, and Clyde was working again, this time for an aircraft parts place, and six days a week. So we were once again solvent for the time being.

On colder days I would pack Lisa in a box on the sled and drag her around for a while, just to get outside. Debbie taught herself to ice skate on a pair of double-bladed skates and spent most of her out-of-doors time each day skating with her other little friends. Lisa loved playing in the snow, and ran around in it like it was nothing at all. They were such good kids, and seemed to be thriving in this type of cold climate.

The days were getting longer, gaining 5 or 6 minutes each day. I could hardly wait for the long days of summer to come again when the fishing, swimming, camping, berry picking and all the outdoor summer things start. We wanted to get on with hunting for a place of our own and get out of the trailer park. It felt cramped and public to us, and I didn't think we could ever get used to living so close to so many people. We also agreed to try to catch enough salmon and can it all to send some to our families Outside.

Chapter 7 The Big Earthquake

I t was Good Friday, March 27th, 1964. I was standing at the stove cooking supper. It was about 5:30 PM. Clyde, Shelley and Debbie were sitting on the couch watching TV, and Lisa was standing near me. Buddy was playing at a neighbor's house. All of a sudden the whole trailer began to shake violently; all I could do was turn the burners off on the gas cook stove and pick Lisa up from where she had been thrown to the floor. We staggered to the couch and sat there while the supper flew off the stove, the glasses and dishes crashed out of the cupboards above the sink and the canisters with sugar, flour, coffee, all the staples, fell off the shelf above the refrigerator, where they had been behind the TV. Of course the lids all popped off the canisters and dumped the contents on top of the spilled dinner and made such an awful mess! The TV didn't fall off the shelf, but the refrigerator, which was under that shelf, and was bolted to the floor was wrenched loose and bounced about two feet out of it's place, leaving big gouges in the tile floor. We couldn't move, the trailer was pitching and twisting so hard. The electricity went off as soon as the shaking started. We heard a loud roaring rumble, and thought we were being bombed; somehow, because of the noise, it didn't register that we were having an earthquake, not at first. We were so scared, we didn't know what to do except pray, hard, and trust in God to make it stop. It lasted over five minutes, and we thought it would never quit. It seemed much longer. Shelley and Debbie cried all through it; Lisa laughed, and Clyde and I just prayed, and hung on to our kids. We could see the ground rolling outside, like large ocean waves. The trees and phone poles were twisting and swaying violently. Other trailers were rising up and down, pitching violently back and forth, and parked cars were rolling back and forth, crashing into each other. The ground cracked in all directions, and through it all was that horrible rumbling roar. We truly thought the world was coming to an end.

When the rolling slowed down, we grabbed the kids and ran outside, after Clyde un-jammed the door. Buddy came running from the neighbor's - they had been outside through it all, hanging on to a fence. We were so relieved! Thank God no one was hurt. Everybody was outside, asking what had happened. I asked our next-door neighbor if he thought we had been bombed, or what? He said no, he thought it was an earthquake. But what a quake. The grand daddy of them all!

Later on we assessed the damage to our trailer, which was only slight, considering the twisting it took. We had no electricity, heat or water until late Saturday night, when we finally got our furnace lit and burning properly, and the electricity went on a little while later. They were still working on the water. It seemed the wonderful artesian well just disappeared. Completely. But they had a standby well, which they would hook up as soon as the water was tested for possible contamination. Meanwhile we melted snow for dishes, and boiled it for drinking. We could not drive anywhere except the short distance to the nearest market and all the water lines were frozen because the power was off for so long. The roads were all in bad shape with broken pavement everywhere. We could not phone our families in the States, because Civil Defense had all the phone lines tied up. We couldn't even send a telegram, since there were no Western Union offices in Spenard and no one was allowed to drive into Anchorage until it was deemed safe to do so. All we could do was send a short special delivery letter when the Post Office opened on Easter Sunday afternoon for a few hours, to our folks and hoped they got it so they wouldn't worry about us. The National Guard was present; to make sure no one tried to drive into town. It was actually about ten days before we could contact our folks. They had frantically called the Red Cross to try to find out if we were okay, and all they found out was that our names were not on a list of injured, missing or dead.

The newscasts on the air in the states had stated that Anchorage was destroyed and that everyone was either dead or injured. We found that out much later, but at the time we had no idea our folks were all so devastated, thinking we had all been killed. All the schools were closed until they had been inspected for damage and the Civil Defense said they could be opened once again. Two schools were totally wrecked.

Easter Sunday morning we went to church dressed in warm pants, sweaters, coats, and warm hats. They had announced over the radio that none of the churches had heat as yet and that everyone should dress warmly. No churches were damaged at all. The next day we all went to our children's' school for typhoid shots, which gave us all very sore arms. The school was okayed to be used, but only for shots, since the heat was not yet on. Two stores were able to open by Easter Sunday afternoon and it was announced on the radio that there was enough food in the supermarket warehouses for a month, and by that time there would be more coming in. We were caught low on everything after the quake, because most of our staple supplies went all over the floor. Also it was the end of the week, and before payday, and I hadn't had a chance to stock up for the next week. But we made do, and others weren't so lucky.

The Easter Bunny did not come and the kids were sad. But there were no eggs left in the store, most of them broke in the earthquake, and the few that were left were sold out before we got there and no Easter baskets and very little candy.

We discovered that we were over a main fault, and that a very deep but narrow crack about two inches wide went under our trailer from front to back and the rest of the trailers in this row, and possibly the water and sewer lines were broken. The landlord thought the sewers were all okay, but he had to dig down to make sure. It turned out that the water lines were broken, but once discovered, were repaired as rapidly as possible. Also the alternate well tested out as good, so in only a few more days we all had water again.

Many people were injured and some killed - it was the worst quake in the history of Alaska. Lots of damage was sustained and some people will never be found. The earth simply opened up and completely swallowed some homes in the Turnagain area; some bars on 4th Avenue sunk to the roof. Searchers found a very happy drunk in one of them -

he thought he had died and gone to heaven - all that booze just for him! For three whole days. They got him out okay, unhurt, but very drunk.

Two boys, age about 13, were in the elevator in the JC Penney store downtown, wrestling and horsing around when the earthquake started. The electricity went off, stranding them between floors; they thought they had broken the elevator, until they forced the door open and managed to squeeze out of the 14-inch crack, and as they were running down the stairs, the walls were caving in behind them. They were very lucky to get out alive, and with no injuries.

A woman was sitting in her parked car on the street in front of Penney's store when the exterior wall fell on her car and crushed her to death.

A man watched his house disappear into the earth with two of his children still inside - what a hopeless feeling that must have been for that poor man, may God have mercy on him.

No one who lived through the earthquake of March 27 at 5:36 PM on Good Friday will ever forget it as long as they live. A lot of people were left homeless, and the tidal waves following the quake actually destroyed the entire town of Valdez, did untold damage to Kodiak, and many people were killed.

The Salvation Army fed and housed over 500 families - about 1460 people or so, and also found or helped to find new places of residence for all of them, within a week. The Lions Club, the American Legion and Moose Lodge all opened their halls to anyone who needed shelter, food and heat, so no one had to go hungry. Also the Post Office began delivering mail again as usual within the week.

The landlord found the breaks in the pipes under the row of trailers we were on. There were three breaks in the water pipes, and the pipes were 8 feet under the ground, and it was a very hard job, digging up all that and fixing the broken pipes. We were so happy to have our water restored once again. We were fortunate, indeed, as most of the people in town weren't able to even use their sewer facilities and the water was badly contaminated there.

Clyde was able to go back to work as soon as the building was declared safe, and he even got a raise. He was parts manager at a sales and service place for small private and semi-private aircraft. They sold parts, engines, planes, and flew freight, homesteaders to their home-sites, sold gas and did repairs.

In spite of everything, we were more determined than ever to stay in Alaska. People were really wonderful. Everyone was bending over backwards to help everyone else. The destruction was terrible. It was all very frightening, and we all tended to panic at the least little tremor, called 'aftershocks', which happened often every day and night. Earthquakes never bothered us before, but now we felt a sense of panic every time a rather strong shock could be felt.

The first time we got into the truck and drove to the store, and the first bumps we hit, Lisa started to scream and cry; we had to stop the truck to calm her down. Delayed reaction, I guess it was, since she laughed all through the quake.

Clyde had to jack the trailer up and re-block it because it bounced all the way off the foundation braces and twisted the skirting, and popped a couple of panels loose on the outside. Once he got the trailer leveled again, the panels slid into place with a little help. Then he fixed the skirting, after the landlord found the breaks in the water pipes, and we only got one storm window cracked out of all that movement. The overhead cabinets in the kitchen pulled away from the wall about an inch, but were easy to re-fasten. That was some sturdy trailer we had - after surviving the Alcan Highway, and then the horrible earthquake, it was still in pretty good shape!

We found that one way to get people to write was to have an earthquake of major proportions. We certainly did receive a lot of mail for about a month or more. People we never expected to hear from wrote to us and we did our best to answer one and all of them.

Major cleanup and rebuilding began at once, and what a stupendous job that was. An ad in the paper read - "NATURAL WONDER FOR SALE - 3 LOTS AND GARAGE, ONLY SELF-RISING LAND IN ALASKA". What a sense of humor! Some folks left Alaska as soon as the roads were open, quite a few, in fact. Kind of like locking the barn after the horse is gone.

About mid-April the weather turned unseasonably warm, and we seemed to be having spring breakup. A lot of mud and water everywhere and rather warm weather, in the mid-40's, shirtsleeve weather. But then, it snowed again, and temperature dropped back down to 25. We thought it was too good to be true. But the same day we received packages from my mom and dad with sweaters for the kids, Easter baskets, and goodies for all. The mail had been delayed because of the earthquake and was slower than ever. But getting those packages cheered us all up.

In May the two youngest, Lisa and Debbie, had been playing with Mac and Frances' kids across the road, who broke out with chicken pox and three weeks later, it was no surprise when our two got it, later in June. The oldest two had already had it, when we were still in Missouri. The weather was very warm and nice and days full of sun once again, and very short dusk nights. So it was an extremely hard chore to keep those two lively ones cooped up inside the house until their spots went away. Neither of them felt sick, except for the first fever, and were as full of pep and energy as usual. One beautiful sunny day while I was ironing in the kitchen and (I thought) the girls were both busy coloring in their bedroom, Debbie went quietly out of the back door and found an old pack of matches. She decided to make herself a campfire in the vacant, brush-filled lot directly behind the trailer. So she piled a few twigs in the grass and lit them. A neighbor, a teenage girl a few doors down had been watching her and ran over to tell me about it. I had to borrow the next-door neighbor's hose to put out the fire, because ours was locked in the tool shed and there wasn't time to unlock the door and hook the hose up. I shudder to think what might have happened if that girl hadn't seen Debbie and what she was up to. There was a breeze blowing and the fire was small, but scattered, and would have rapidly spread to the woods at the back end of the field and no telling where it could have gone from there. When kids get bored, they think up the most mischief, it seems. I was worn out by the time they were all recovered. I was especially glad when Debbie was all recovered and could go to kindergarten the first week of July, for six weeks. Then she could start first grade in the fall, and go to school with the other two school age kids.

We kept getting letters from friends and relatives asking why we weren't moving back since the quake. We told everyone that asked that we weren't coming back. We thought it kind of silly to run away because of the earthquake. No matter where you go in this world there is always something - tornadoes, hurricanes, floods or droughts, - there is nowhere except heaven where one can be perfectly safe. Everything seemed to be measured from that time on by the phrase "since the earthquake". We heard the term so often it seemed.

Mac got out of the Air Force and their family left Alaska for their home in Tennessee about the first of June. We surely missed them. They were such nice people.

Anchorage had and still has quite a transient population, mainly because of the military bases, but partly because of the long winters. Some folks just can't seem to take the length of time the snow is on the ground and the long periods of cold weather, with no clear cut signs of fall or spring. The saying is 'Alaska has two seasons, Little Winter and Big Winter'. Also, it seems to be a place one either loves, or hates. No middle ground. And we loved it.

Chapter 8   Happier Times

C lyde got another raise, and to celebrate, after Church the next Sunday, which happened to be sunny and beautiful, we went with some friends to Wasilla Lake and had a picnic, and fished a little. We were so happy, and I know the kids were too, to finally be able to go whenever we wanted to, since the two youngest were finally over their spots and no longer had to be confined to the house. What a relief!!

We continued to hunt for some land for ourselves. Because Clyde was working six days a week, it was hard to find enough time to go anyplace, but we had everything ready to be packed in the truck as soon as he got home from work, on Saturdays, and took off right away for whatever destination we had planned. We would stop and have a picnic supper on the way, and by doing that, and spending the night in the truck, we were able to look around more. Then during the week, whenever Clyde could get a little bit of time off, added to his lunch hour, he would go to the land office and find out what ever he could about any land available, such as a home site, or homestead land. Unfortunately the people at the land office weren't very helpful, or forthcoming with information, so it was slow going. Before too long, however, Clyde had enough actual information to know that the Federal homesteads were all taken up within 200 miles of Anchorage along any road, and the State had whatever land was left, with none offered at that time. It was too bad that my car was dead, or I could have saved him the time and trouble. But such is life.

Debbie had finally started kindergarten, and liked it very much. She brought home the most fantastic pictures; I thought then that perhaps she would be an artist when she grew up. In actual fact, she went on, after graduating from high school, to College and got an Associates Degree in Art. She is quite talented.

Grizzly bears were seldom found in the lower climes of Alaska, according to the radio. However, one came down out of the mountains and was making a general nuisance of himself and a hunter shot him just a mile from where we lived. The bear stood over eight feet tall!

We caught some rainbow trout in Campbell Creek, just a mile up the road, and they were simply delicious. It spurred us on to continue our hunt. Clyde got the weekend off, and we planned to camp out all weekend at Montana Creek up above Wasilla. This was the third weekend of July, in 1964. We had a glorious weekend, hot and sunny. We took off as soon as Clyde got home from work, after packing the camper with food and clothes and bedding, and drove to Montana Creek, about 120 miles north of Anchorage. We got there about 9:30 PM, and found a good place to park, about 100 yards from the water, in what used to be a construction camp. There were boarded up wells and sewer pipes all over the place. We built a fire and had dinner. Of course it was still light, but dusk was just beginning to settle in. After dinner I tacked some bath towels over the windows in the camper, since the curtains weren't heavy enough to keep out the light, and we all went to bed. Clyde woke me up about 4:30 am, and he and I went outside and made a fire again, and I cooked up a batch of hotcakes and a pot of coffee, and did that ever taste good! Then Clyde walked down to the creek, where there were about six or seven cars and campers, nearer the water. But we had the place where we were parked all to ourselves. Clyde fished for a while, but didn't catch a thing. The kids stayed asleep until about 8:00. Meanwhile I just enjoyed sitting by the fire and sipping hot coffee, soaking in the peace and quiet. It was chilly, but the sun was shining; it came up about 2 am at that time in the summer.

When the kids were up, I made their breakfasts of hotcakes, and cleaned out the camper. Then we went exploring and found a whole patch of rhubarb that must have been planted by the construction crew, or someone. I picked nearly all of it, and put the stalks in a plastic bag to take home and fix a pie or two.

Bud went fishing for a while with Clyde and some of the campers by the creek got up and told Clyde they hadn't had any luck either. We decided to move on after a while. We drove up to Talkeetna, about 40 miles farther north, and stopped at a lake on the way that looked promising. By that time it was hot and the kids went swimming while Clyde fished. The lake wasn't deep and had a stream running into it where we stopped. The kids splashed around and found lots of mussel shells. The water was cool, but not cold, except in the stream. That was icy. Clyde fished in his hip boots way over by some lily pads. There were all kinds of big trout laying in the sun and swimming lazily by his feet, but they wouldn't bite at all. If we had a dip net, he could have just reached down and scooped them up.

Shortly after we left there, we drove back to Montana Creek Lodge to fill up our water jugs, and while we were doing that, we met a couple of men working on the construction crew building the Susitna River Bridge, past Talkeetna. They told us about a little known road that went to another branch of Montana Creek, where king salmon were laying around in deep holes.

They said they caught their limit in trout up there. So we turned around once again and went back towards Talkeetna, found the road (if you could call it that) and drove two and a half miles into the woods where the road was washed out by the earlier floods at the edge of the creek. There was a nice wide spot to park, all sand and gravel, and the men who had told us about the place had followed us in and showed Clyde where to go to find the best pools to fish. They told us that no one was permitted to catch a king salmon that year; if you did, you had to throw it back. If you didn't, and got caught with one, it was a $500 fine.

I set up camp while Clyde went with the two men to fish for trout. The kids all got busy and helped gather sticks for firewood, and rocks for a fire ring. We found some logs to use as seats around the fire. When the fire was going well, I put out all the food. We had brought along a chicken to cook, and I cut it in half, washed it in the creek, put salt and pepper on it and a pat of butter and wrapped each half up in foil, then set it on the grate over the hot coals to cook slowly. We had hot dogs for lunch by the lake, and the chicken would be for supper.

The kids had a wonderful time playing in the sand and splashing in a shallow part of the creek, dipping the fishing poles in and watching baby trout nibble on the bait.

Clyde came back in a little while with three large beautiful trout. One was a rainbow, and the other two were dolly varden. He was just beaming from ear to ear and a little bit later the two men came back with one grayling and a 15 pound king salmon, which they wrapped up in a tarp and hid in the spare tire well of their station wagon, and then drove away. We offered to feed the men, but they were in a hurry to get back to camp. And so we ate our delicious chicken, pork and beans, the rest of the potato salad left from lunch, sweet and dill pickles, canned tomatoes and fresh fried trout. They were superb!

After eating, Clyde and Bud went off to fish some more, and this time Clyde took the big gun along because where there's salmon, there's nearly always bear, and he saw some really fresh bear tracks where he had been fishing earlier. This time Bud caught a nice big four-pound rainbow, and was he ever proud; the biggest fish he had ever caught in his young life, so far, and Clyde had a real thrill too, when he caught a 40-pound king, which went under a log and snapped his line just like that! He said it nearly pulled him into the water. He was so excited about the fishing; he said we would just spend another night right there. So we did.

Bud after catching his first rainbow trout!

Clyde had left the plastic sack of salmon eggs for bait on a sand bar about 100 feet upstream from our camp, and he forgot to go back and get them. In the morning when he went to look for them, they were gone, and there were fresh bear tracks. He caught three more rainbow, and we packed them in the icebox, ate the lunch I had already fixed and got ready to go home. Earlier we had discovered we were all out of mosquito repellent, and the mosquitoes sure knew it right away, and spread the word. We were all eaten up by the time we finished lunch, packed up and cleaned up our camp area.

We arrived home about 6:30 pm, and I cooked the rest of the trout for supper. We certainly enjoyed ourselves, except for the mosquitoes, which were worse there than anyplace we had ever been. The next day we were all a mass of itchy lumps from all the bites we had sustained. We loved the looks of the country up by Montana Creek and Talkeetna area. It is gorgeous, as is most of Alaska.

On the road, which was reminiscent of the Alcan Highway in parts, we could see Mt. McKinley, with just a wisp of cloud hanging over the tip. What a mountain! It is certainly awe-inspiring; brings about stillness to the spirit, as you gaze at all that concentrated beauty. Coming around the bend, there it would be, seeming to leap into the sky all of a sudden. I can understand why so many people have this driving urge to climb it, but I would rather be here on the ground enjoying the view.

The last Sunday of July we went to Portage Glacier. It was a beautiful day, but the highway was awful. It was extremely torn up and badly in need of repair. On the way back from Portage Glacier, we stopped at Bird Creek and caught five nice salmon.

We had been using any and all spare time searching for 'our' place, but so far everything we saw and tried to file on seemed to be already taken by the State, and no one could file on State land at that time. But at last we finally found out, in spite of the lack of helpfulness of the people in the Federal land office. It was like pulling teeth from a tiger to get any helpful answers. Of course we realized it would help if we knew just what to ask, but we learned by trial and error. We continued to search.

The
Dream

Chapter 9   The Dream

Armed with maps and information, at last, Clyde discovered that the State had taken all the land up to 20 miles north of Talkeetna on any existing road. It seemed that the next thing was the railroad, and since it was still Federal land, and available for homesteading, he went down to the depot and bought himself a ticket to Sherman, which was well north, of where the State had taken over, according to the maps obtained from the land office. The place he picked, thinking it was a small town, was really only a railroad siding. It was a beautiful little valley. He got off the train, looked around and began walking out into the weeds, on a flat piece of land, and very shortly he came to a place, an indentation where the weeds had all been flattened down, and a fresh pile of steaming bear droppings. Even though he had never been close enough to smell bear, he was positive that one had been there, just then; nothing else smelled like that. He rapidly turned and retraced his steps, and headed north on the railroad tracks. He discovered there was a booth, actually a railroad dispatch phone booth.

Bud Lovel at the Phone Shack at the South Switch at Sherman

He walked north about half mile or so and saw a flat roof peeking over the weeds, just visible from the tracks. It turned out to be a little two-room shack, and an old woman came running out and yelled for him to come on in and visit for a while. She had coffee ready and cookies, and much information. Her name was Dixie Rudder, and her husband, Wally was on his way home from Fairbanks, where he had been working. She told Clyde that they had filed seven years before on

160 acres to homestead, but all they managed to get done was to build the house out of old lumber salvaged from what used to be a railroad section house across the tracks from them, next to the creek. They had relinquished their claim, and the property was no longer listed on the Federal maps as taken. Dixie told Clyde they were getting ready to move to Washington State, and the day before had been the last day of Wally's job. She said the reason they never finished proving up on the place was because Wally had a bad heart. She told him they would be moving around the middle or end of September. They had three beautiful sled dogs, named Johnnie, George, and Suzie, and they trapped all winter through the mountain passes a few miles back of their place every year to make part of the money they needed to live out there. She seemed very lonely, Clyde told me, and certainly talked a mile a minute about everything. They lived out there all those years without a phone, a neighbor, or anything.

When it came time for the south bound train, Clyde and Dixie went out to meet it, and when Clyde waved his jacket, it stopped, and Wally got off, and Clyde visited with him for a few minutes before getting on the train to come back to town. He managed to find out lots of information, both from the Rudders and from the trainmen. When he got home he told me about his great adventure, and that he planned to go again the following weekend and take me up there to see the place and if I liked it as well as he did, we could pick out some land and stake it and perhaps we could actually get moved in before winter set in.

Originally we had planned to get land by a road, so the kids could continue to go to school, but it didn't seem likely because we could not afford to buy land at that time. But Dixie told Clyde about the Correspondence Study Program in Juneau, available to all bush people, and that some of the folks at Gold Creek, were home teaching their kids. It seemed there were four or five homesteads and a railroad section house at Gold Creek, just five miles north of Sherman. And so we talked far into the night, and all week as well, making plans.

During the week, I arranged for someone to take care of the kids for the following weekend, and packed what I thought we would need to camp out overnight. We included some fresh fruit for Dixie and Wally, because Clyde said Dixie had mentioned to him that they never seemed to have enough fresh fruit, but didn't have much problem with fresh vegetables in summer, from the small garden she planted. Also in the seven years they had lived at Sherman, they had only been to Anchorage three times!

Clyde had tentatively picked out land bordering the Rudder's old boundary, to the south, and if I approved, he would file on it. So we boarded the train, and took off for Sherman. That was a fascinating experience, my first ride on a train in Alaska.

We got off by the creek on the north end of the Rudder's place, and wandered up the path to the house. It meandered from the tracks, through a little patch of woods, past a pile of old boards and timber, up through the nearly head high-weeds, through a little garden patch. Of course the Rudders had come down the path as soon as the train stopped, and met us about half way. They were overjoyed to get the fresh fruit and invited us to eat a meal with them. Dixie said she would give us the old couch and chair, their wood cook stove, and a folding bed, to help us get started. One of their dogs was sick, and they asked us if we could pick up some medicine and send it to them on the train, when we got back to town, which we did. After lunch, Clyde and I left to go scout out what would be "our" place, if I liked it and thought I could live there.

We walked south on the railroad tracks, and really liked the look of it all. What I had seen from the train, all the way from Talkeetna I liked, so it came as no surprise that the acreage Clyde had picked out seemed made to order. There was mostly flat land and fairly level in the front part, with a lot of trees and lush grass, actually native plants, weeds, clear up to my head. The land rose gradually into benches, and on the first bench, about 1/3 mile from the tracks were a lot of brushy trees, short, and some tall timber mixed in as well. Each low bench had more trees than the last, and was steeper, until the trees ran out and there were only alders, and bare mountain tops. It was all beautiful.

So we picked out our 160 acres, with a mountain spring flowing right through the center of it, under the railroad tracks, and into the Susitna River on the other side of the tracks. The railroad used that spring, where they had a pool dug out near the tracks, for their water supply in the winter, as it never freezes. They would fill the water cars for the roving gangs as needed. It was a wonderful weekend of exploring, staking, marking and trying to get it all straight and get it all done before taking the train back to Anchorage. We were worn out

Saturday night and slept like logs. The bears could have eaten us both, and we would not have noticed that's how tired we were. Actually we did see signs of bear, but not very fresh. Anyway, we had the big gun, as I called it, with us. It was a 30-06, so I felt safe. We discovered the plentiful array of berries of different types, and there were high bush cranberries, all over the place, a few patches here and there of low bush cranberries, which were just like the commercial type, except tiny and few and hard to find. There were also currants, rosehips and up on the higher benches there were blueberries. Also wild raspberries, and salmon berries, wild strawberries, very small and sparse, like the low bush cranberries.

On Sunday, after we finished all our labors, we hiked back up to the Rudder's place and told them what we had done and what we planned to do. Dixie told me she had strawberries planted in her yard, and rhubarb and she would give me some of each to plant on our place. "OUR PLACE", imagine!!! Dixie and Wally told us there were moose and black bear, also ptarmigan, and spruce hen. Up in the hills there were caribou herds and grizzly bear. Beaver, muskrat, ermine, mink and other valuable fur bearing animals were plentiful, according to Dixie. Her collection of furs was beautiful.

We had such a short time to get ready for winter that we were panicky, and I sent special delivery letters to all our folks, soon as we got back to town and gathered up the kids and put them to bed. The letters were short, describing the place and what we planned and begging them, anybody, for loans of money, in whatever amount they could spare, to help us pay freight, and buy materials and supplies, and get going. We had been so busy paying off bills; we did not have any savings, or extra money at all, actually.

Clyde filed at the land office right away, and paid the filing fees, and when we found out about the freight, he brought the lumber and other things we had been gathering for the last months to the freight depot. Among the things we had to ship were sheets of plywood taken from an old burned out trailer we bought. We had salvaged the lean-to, which had not been burned, and had two by fours, an aluminum room, called a cabana, which we had brought up the Alcan packed into the living room of our trailer, among other things. It had all been stacked neatly behind the trailer and covered with canvas tarps just waiting for this occasion.

Curry house, Alaska

Our nearest neighbors, once Dixie and Wally moved away, would be five miles to the north at Gold Creek and ten miles to the south at Curry with no one for 150 miles east and west, as far as we knew. I was hoping the Rudders would somehow change their minds and stay. The passenger train came by twice a day in summer; one north bound and one south bound. Anyone could wave their arm, or a jacket or something and flag it down. It would stop anywhere. There also were freight trains running at different times night and day.

The nearest hospital was 90 miles away, in Palmer, and the nearest town was Talkeetna, 32 miles to the south, and also the end of the road, which was gravel. It was a five-hour trip by train from Anchorage to Sherman. Our mail, unless it was urgent, would all go to Gold Creek, where there was a railroad section house and five or six homesteads, five miles north. The section foreman came down in a track car to deliver the mail, Dixie told us. If you marked it 'urgent' and addressed it to Sherman, the train would blow the whistle three times, and you were supposed to come out to the tracks, and they would tie a rock on to the big brown mail envelope it would be put in and toss it out of the baggage car door. The rock was used to weigh it down so it would not blow under the train and become confetti.

The Alaska Rail Road was really unique. It stopped anywhere, for anyone waving their arm or a shirt or anything; a real "Toonerville Trolley" type. It swayed from side to side, creaked, groaned and jerked; but they got there on time, (sort of) and made a profit besides, we were told, even though the rates were low. On our way back to Anchorage they had to stop and wait for a moose to get off the tracks and we saw a black bear on the other side of the Susitna River standing on his hind legs watching the train. It was all very exciting. The conductor told us that all the sidings were named after a place or person.

The following weekend we again took the train, and when we got to Sherman, the train stopped at the north siding, and dumped off our lumber and we dragged it off through the weeds to the spot we had picked out for the house. We set up camp, and left our pack boards and sleeping bags. We knew we had to hurry back and get started on some sort of foundation for a small cabin to do us through the winter. We would need to recruit more help, of course as soon as possible in order to get a dwelling up before winter. We knew not what we did, at that point, but were just blundering along there. And so we hiked up to the Rudder's cabin, and took the box of food we had brought along with us, as we did not want to leave it for the bears to get into. They thought we weren't coming because the train didn't stop by their house. Dixie had already fixed dinner for us and when the train didn't stop, they went ahead and ate. So they were surprised when we came up the path. Dixie, a great cook, had fixed plenty, and so we ate, and while we were eating they insisted that we sleep in their house and not out with the bears, and also told us that they had been talking it over and decided that we could have the house if we wanted to buy it from them, as they were just going to leave it anyway. Wow! What a break! They said we should just go and change the filing at the land office right away, and re-file enclosing the house within our new land boundaries.

We negotiated an equally satisfactory price for the house, which included a gasoline washing machine, (which needed work) and one of the sled dogs, a harness and a dogsled. All of which needed repair of some sort including the dog. Suzie, the dog that had been sick, was then better, but very shy and timid, not having been around people much in her short life. We thought then that if she didn't make friends with the kids, we would keep her strictly for a watchdog and also to haul in firewood and moose meat, in the winter. At that point, we certainly had a lot to learn!

While Clyde went to move the front boundary stakes we had set the weekend before, Dixie took me all over her yard, showing me where the strawberry patch was located, under a mass of weeds, but nevertheless with silver dollar sized strawberries, and her patch of rhubarb, also under masses of weeds, five big plants. Then she showed me where there was a patch of wild chives, and also a wild cucumber plant, which was unique. In the spring, she said, you take the tender leaves, stem and all, and chop them up in a salad. They taste just like cucumber. Then you take the same plant and cook it like spinach; it tastes like asparagus. When the berries are ripe in late summer or fall, they taste like watermelon and can be eaten raw, or cooked with other berries for juice or jelly. What a versatile plant! She showed me how to identify wild rhubarb and told me many things about the wild edible plants, which I tried to write down so I could remember it all. Much later on, I had to buy a book describing, and with pictures, the wild and edible plants of Alaska.

Everything seemed to be going in our favor at that point, so we thought that was what must have been in the Master Plan for us. The Railroad freight office charged us $10.00 for the 700 pounds of lumber we took up with us. All of that was down at the other end of the property, not even on the part we had filed on, once Clyde reset the front stakes. I guess that was "excess baggage", since it came up on the passenger train with us. We still had all the rest of the freight coming, whenever Clyde had it all down there to ship, from the actual freight house. It would be shipped only when we were finally moved up, and had the paperwork from the land office stating that our filing was valid. It would be a few weeks, probably as much as six weeks yet, at that time. But since we had a house, we didn't have to worry about erecting a shelter before winter.

We were so excited by all the new changes. We made plans with the Rudders, since they wanted to move out and be gone to Washington in about three weeks or so, we set a date right then and there, for me and the kids to come up, and since it would be in the middle of the week, they assured Clyde that they would have plenty of wood and so forth laid by to last until the weekend when he could come up. He would have to go on working and just come up weekends until he could sell the trailer and truck.

Dixie told us we had better be sure to get there before they left, because some folks at Gold Creek had their eyes on the windows, and whatever else was useable, to salvage. Dixie assured us she would inform them by mail if no other way, that the house and all in it was spoken for.

The house needed a new roof, since it leaked like a sieve. It was flat, and flat roofs tend to do that in this country - the ice builds up and breaks through the tarpaper, and that's all it takes. The rudders had buckets here and there to catch the leaks.

The house was small, only two rooms with windows set low in the walls, for some reason, and one door, at the back of the house, facing the woods to the east. Most of the time we were there we spent outside re-staking the boundary lines, putting up our marker posts, measuring and beating our way through the tall grass and brush to where we were trying to go. We were worn out and glad to get back on the train. We barely spent any time in the house, except to grab a quick bite, and to sleep. It was a hard two days, once again. But on the way back we saw two black bear cubs playing on the bank of the Susitna River, and a few miles further two moose near a creek; also a lot of dead salmon laying around in little creeks, and two beaver working on their dam. What a show! As well as a herd of caribou near Eagle Flats the day before.

Clyde went down to the land office the next day and re-filed, changing the description of our land, and enclosing the creek to the north of the house. So then we had a creek running through the north end of the property, as well as the spring running through the middle, about, and the land enclosed more flat country, and less mountain. An oblong shape, running along the Railroad boundary.

We were so excited and thrilled that the adrenaline rush kept us going for long hours every day, packing, planning, telling the kids everything, making lists. Clyde went up with a friend from work and put a new roof on the house, a slanted one, and brought some other things with him that we would need when we got moved up.

The next two weeks we fixed and hauled; we made a barrel stove for heat, out of a heavy 55 gallon gas drum and cast iron fittings we bought for it, which consisted of legs, a collar for the chimney to fit in, and a door to load wood into. We tried it out in the yard to see how it would work, and it was fine. Clyde bought a small propane gas cook range at the GSA sales on the base, of surplus government stuff, and took it down and had it steam cleaned. He hauled those stoves and lots of heavy lumber and supplies to the freight depot, to store with the rest of our stuff there, until ready to ship.

The kids and I hopped the train Tuesday, September 8th, 1964 to move up here. We had beds, trunks, food, clothes, dishes, pans, all the things we would need for the time being, until the bulk of our stuff came on the local freight. That's the only freight during the week, which would stop and drop supplies off for homesteaders and residents along the railroad. All the other freights went straight through to Fairbanks.

The passenger train baggage car carried everything imaginable, from regular luggage to sled dogs, roofing material, doors, skis, sleds, groceries, cans of gas, lumber, windows, bedding - just about anything. Sometimes you had to pay a fee - what they called "excess baggage", but it wasn't very much. There was a baggage man taking care of everything and helping people load and unload at each stop. The local freight brought all the really heavy stuff, like drums of gasoline, propane tanks, furniture, bulky items, and long large things, which wouldn't fit into a baggage car on the passenger train.

Chapter 10 Life on the Homestead

W hen the kids and I got off the train, it was raining a little, but clearing up. Only then, after we got off, did I realize how dangerous it might be for the kids. Seeing them standing on the ground, with the weeds so high, I could see that one step off the path would swallow up any one of them, especially Lisa, who was only two years old, and not very tall. I knew that the most important thing was to get them to the house right away and then figure out what to do from there. It was their first train ride, and they all loved it.

Early homestead 1967

The train stopped by the path, which came out of a little patch of woods, down by the bridge over the creek. It meandered through the woods, and around the strawberry patch, up a little hill and to the house, which was also buried in weeds. I could just see the roof above the top of the weeds.

We also brought a short haired watch dog named Took, since Suzie died, I knew we would need some warning in case a bear came along. Each child had a box or bag to carry, and I followed in the rear with Took on a leash, and the rifle, watching that none of the kids got off the path. We made our way through soggy weeds that were over my head, and I was relieved when Wally and Dixie met us part way and helped with the bags. We made it to the house, finally.

When we got inside, the first thing I noticed was the plastic hanging from the ceiling, wall to wall, in both rooms. Each room had a big garbage pail in the center of the room, with a string hanging down from the middle of the plastic sheet, and a stream of water flowing down the string into the garbage pail. Seems like the roof leaked worse than ever since Clyde put the new one on top of the old. He forgot to close in the edges and all the rain that blew in formed puddles on the sagging under roof, and came through all the new nail holes. So then we had running water in the house, as well.

It didn't seem like the path to the tracks should have been so long, but when I asked Dixie about it, she said that they couldn't make one straight down to the tracks because there was a real deep ditch down next to the tracks and it would be too tough to climb up and down the ditch. They made the path where it was because the old shack (and it was a shack!) was built out of lumber torn out of the old section house across the tracks near the creek.

They hauled the lumber over by the trail, and that was where the trail stayed. The rest of the section house that wasn't used in building the cabin was dumped in the middle of the little patch of woods; they called it the 'wood dump'. (On closer inspection, there were old, wet, half - rotten boards, plasterboard chunks, rusty nails, old water-soaked doors; all of that grown up in weeds for years.)

The next thing I noticed, while we were eating lunch, which Dixie had ready for us (bless her heart), was that there was no door in the doorway; just a moth-eaten old Army blanket hanging over the hole, where there once was a door, at least it was there the last time I was there. I asked Wally what happened to the door, and he said, "Oh, the old door broke when the big old tree fell on the house last week so we used the door for firewood. But there's doors down at the wood dump." Oh yes. Then I asked Wally if any other damage was done to the house by the tree, and he said, "Oh, a beam was cracked, not much else. Some folks come by and cut up the big old tree into hunks and moved it away from the doorway so's we could get outside. Only the top of the tree fell on the house, but it hit the door purty hard."

When I asked about bears getting in, Dixie said she didn't think I would have to worry, with the dogs barking and all; but there was one bear, (she said) which liked to climb up the big tree near the front corner of the house and tease the dogs by waving its' front paw at them. (OH DEAR GOD)!

Of course, I had the 30-06 and plenty of shells if I needed to shoot, and with Took and Johnnie, (Dixie said we could have him instead of Suzie, since she died), we should have plenty of warning if any bears came around. The dogs really barked loudly, and were chained to the house and slept under the house. The two dogs the Rudders had left were Johnnie, and George, his papa, who was also promised to someone in Gold Creek. George was pure white, beautiful and huge.

Dixie told me that Johnnie was a good sled dog and probably would be better with the kids than Suzie would have been. He was a MacKenzie River Husky, a reddish brown color, with mean looking yellow wolf's eyes. He was fastened to the front of the house by a chain, and George was chained to the north side of the house. We tied Took to the south, near the open doorway. The other two dogs wanted to kill poor Took on sight, even though he wasn't full grown and was smaller than either of the huskies.

I thought the Rudders were staying on until the weekend, so Dixie could show me how to cook on the wood cookstove, how to build hot enough fires to be able to cook on it, and where to get firewood, and all the things I needed to know to survive out there. But then Dixie told me that a neighbor from Gold Creek was walking down later that day to help them load the boxes and barrels of stuff they had packed and piled up all over the house, down to the tracks for the freight to pick up, and that they planned to take the train the next day, September 9th, to Anchorage. I nearly panicked right then and was really tempted to take the train the next day also, except that I hadn't brought any money along. Where would I spend money out there?

Oh, how I longed for Clyde!! We had only been there for about two hours, and I felt absolutely overwhelmed. Clyde couldn't come with us because he had to work. He thought we would be fine until the weekend, when he would come up, and, (he thought) when the Rudders were leaving.

After lunch Dixie kept Debbie and Lisa in the house while Shelley, Bud and I went back down to the tracks to haul all the rest of our stuff up to the house. They stayed close to me and were a real help, even though neither of them could lift very heavy objects yet, we managed. Wally helped me set up the bunk beds for the kids, and pretty soon the man came down from Gold Creek and carried all the heavy barrels and boxes down to the tracks, and there was more room in the house. Then he left and I couldn't remember his name since he wasn't there long enough to talk to, and worked the whole time he was there. He took George with him when he left.

We were exhausted, and slept like logs the first night. The next morning, which was Wednesday, I asked Wally if he would help me hang a door. I knew nothing whatsoever about hanging doors. He told me if I could get one of the doors up from the wood dump he would help me hang it. Well, there was only one door that I could find all in one piece, and I wished I had known how heavy it was the day before - I would have asked the neighbor for help. I swear that door weighed 150 pounds if it weighed an ounce. It was soaked, and I struggled for nearly two hours with both Bud and Shelley helping me, through all those weeds, to the house. And then Wally said it was the wrong size and he couldn't do anything about it. He said it was too tall and skinny for the door opening. But he promised if I would write a note to Clyde that he'd get it to Clyde and that he could bring a door up on Saturday.

Believe me, I wrote a note, and a long one, and measured the door opening as well, and then it was time, all of a sudden, to learn how to build a fire in the cookstove, and learn how to cook on it and in the oven, and it was such a fast lesson, I hoped I could remember. Which was the damper, and which was the draft? Which did I pull and which did I push? How could I tell if it was open or closed? Oh boy.

It also turned out that there was no "woodpile," only the old sodden lumber in the lumber dump, and I'd have to chop it all up for firewood if I wanted to cook anything at all.

By the time Wally and Dixie got dressed in their 'town clothes' and put their old longhaired black tomcat in his cage and got the cage of birds covered, it was train time and the kids and I helped carry their stuff down to the tracks and waved goodbye. And there we were - all alone in the wilderness. I almost fell apart at the seams right there.

All four kids and I got to work; the house was a mess and everything needed to be done before we could go to bed again. Thank goodness the sun was shining, and the mosquitoes weren't too bad that day. We made a game out of it. Bud helped me block the doorway with one of our trunks so Lisa wouldn't wander out, and I opened a couple of windows, and we set to work. And it was work!

We hauled out all the dirty clothes they had left behind; underneath those were some gunny sacks with a few rotten potatoes in each; small piles where the old tom cat hadn't made it outside in time; and piled it all up outside for burning later on.

When we found the floor, (a plain board floor, with cracks between each board for dirt to settle in, which badly needed paint or some sort of covering) we swept, carried, threw out, scrubbed with Lysol, bleach and laundry detergent, then rinsed, using up all the roof water from both barrels. We cleaned a place in the kitchen by the window and shoved the big old couch in there. It would be our living room also. I had Shelley watch Lisa, while Bud, Debbie and I hauled everything out to the dump behind the house, got rid of it once and for all, and found enough buckets for hauling water.

Then we all trooped down to the creek; I carried the rifle - I hoped I hadn't ruined my kids for life, but I told them if they stepped off the path into the tall weeds, a bear would instantly eat them. I also told them if they didn't stay right next to me at all times that the same thing would happen. The only one I was really worried about was Lisa. She was so small, and she was too young to understand any of the dangers involved. I'm sure I was over-reacting, but at that time it was a matter of life and death to me, and I was scared stiff, not really knowing what to expect, and after listening to all Dixie's bear tales wondering what in the world I had been thinking of to expose my children to such dangers. But it was too late to do anything about that, we were there and we just had to make the best of it.

We made six trips to the creek; even Lisa had her little bucket of water to carry; then we were so hungry we couldn't stand it any longer. So came the moment of truth - build a fire in the old cookstove and cook dinner. Right. The only firewood there was happened to be down at the old wood dump, and none of it was chopped up into stove-size pieces; most of it was down under the weeds, and wet. I got a box of it chopped up with a dull old ax I found in the weeds, and tried to build a fire. All the stove would do was smoke. I fiddled with the levers and things, but forgot what Dixie had said they were for; finally, out of desperation, I opened a can of Spam and we had sandwiches and a dish of fruit and the kids were all ready to go to bed, they were so tired. We used up all the bread - what on earth would we do all the rest of the week if I couldn't make that dumb stove work?

Before I went to bed, I stacked the trunks on top of each other to block the doorway and piled empty tin cans on top of a rickety folding chair, so if anything tried to get in during the night it would make such a racket we would be sure to wake up. Then I tried to close the window above my bed; the whole thing fell in, right on the bed, casing and all, leaving a big gaping hole in the wall. It was getting dark, so I found a hammer and a few old rusty nails, and put the window casing back in the hole and jammed a nail in each side to try to hold the window in. And said my prayers, lots of times. I fell asleep with the loaded rifle next to me in the bed on one side and Lisa on the other. We didn't have a bed for her yet.

That first evening, all the kids wanted to feed the dogs, but I wouldn't let them near Johnnie until I got up the courage to get close to him myself. He looked so vicious, like he wanted to eat you up, and was so big with those mean looking eyes. He jumped and barked all the time. While the kids watched from a safe distance, I eased a pan of food to him with a stick, and when he finished eating, I gave him a pan of fresh water. His tail was wagging, which I hoped meant he liked me, and I ventured a pat. It turned out he was a very friendly dog, and hadn't been given much attention. All he wanted was to be played with and petted. When I let the kids come near, he sat down and wagged all over and let them pet him, and he licked them all thoroughly and loved it. So that was a real plus. However, I made it clear to the kids that they weren't to come near him unless I was right there, just in case he decided to turn vicious. Took, of course, was still tied by the back doorway; I thought maybe he'd be able to discourage any bears that happened along.

The next morning we did something about the weeds in the yard. We found a rusty old scythe and a couple of empty, rusty old fuel barrels and got to work. I told the kids to yell and scream and make all the noise they could and to have a good time, and we would play a game of roll the barrel. It worked very well; they took turns rolling around on the old barrels and got a sizable portion of the weeds flattened. I had the rifle strapped on, of course and used the scythe. Finally we all got so hot in the blazing sun we had to go in where it was cooler and have some Kool-Aid; I messed with the stove and really got it to burn, finally - I guess the wood got dry enough- and heated some soup for lunch. I tried to make a pan of biscuits. It didn't work. The oven didn't get hot enough to do more than just warm the dough. It was Bud's eighth birthday, September 10th, and our first full day all alone on the homestead - I couldn't even bake Bud a cake!

After lunch we went out to find the strawberry patch. I knew it was under the weeds somewhere; all the kids helped, except Lisa, and she fell asleep. Finally we found the patch, which was full of strawberries just like Dixie said, and they were big, juicy and pale pink, sort of salmon colored, and sweeter than any I'd ever tasted. Probably because we were all still hungry. Soup alone was not enough, considering the physical work we all had done. We picked a big bowl full, took them back to the house, and fixed them with a little sugar. Bud got the biggest bowl full, instead of a birthday cake. I promised him we'd have a real party when his Dad came home on Saturday.

We finished the day cleaning and scrubbing the kitchen. The only thing in the kitchen was the stove, some empty wooden kerosene crates, a rickety table with one leg missing, and a couple of rickety wooden folding chairs and the old couch we had moved in there the day before. There were no cupboards, shelves, no sink, no countertops, or anything, just four walls, two windows, and a doorway hung with the old holey Army blanket. Everything we had brought with us was still packed in boxes and trunks, with no place to put the pans, dishes, or any of the canned or boxed food. So we made some shelves out of the old wooden kerosene crates. They were all dirty too, but we took them outside into the hot sun and scrubbed them with a stiff brush, soap and water and let them dry in the sun. Then I nailed them to the wall in the corner and put the dishes and pans in them. I found an old 2 by 4 board in the yard that was about the right size and used it to prop up the broken leg on the table after we pushed it against the middle wall. Even though it sagged a little on one end, it was fairly sturdy, and some place to put the dishpans while washing dishes, which we didn't have to do yet, thank God.

We found and hauled in more fire wood and stacked it up in boxes around the stove, and got some more water-logged wood from the wood dump to put by the little tin sheepherders stove in the bedroom, which I hadn't had to use yet because it hadn't been cold enough to need a fire in there. Meanwhile, every time the dogs barked, we looked out at the old tree in front to see if a bear was in it or not.

We found some more old tree branches, dragged them to the house and broke them up for firewood. The kids finally got tired of working and had figured out that it wasn't fun anymore. Besides, they were starving, even though they'd been eating everything in sight ever since we got there; they were hungry all the time.

We went inside and I tried to cook again on the old wood cookstove; I wished again that I had brought more food, especially bread. I longed for our old camp stove, anything that would cook. I knew that old woodstove would cook, for Dixie turned out some really fine meals on it. The trouble was me. I had never before in my life used one of those, and it defeated me. But I was determined to find out how it worked one way or another. I got the fire going, heated up a couple of cans of stew, and hoped the biscuits would finally bake. The dough was getting stale, sitting in the oven all that time. I kept shoving more and more wood in the fire, and the stove got hotter and hotter, but the biscuits didn't bake, so I took the pan out of the oven and put it on the stove top, and let them brown that way, and then turned them over. They were the worst biscuits I had ever made - dried out, hard and scorched on the outside, soggy and raw inside, and those poor kids gobbled every one of them down to the last crumb. They complained that they were still hungry, so I opened a big can of pork and beans, fixed some instant mashed potatoes, and finally filled them up.

All the time we were eating dinner, water was heating on the stove, which I kept stuffing wood into; it sure burned wood fast! All the kids got a bath in the old round washtub that was hanging on a nail by the back porch, one at a time, of course, but they were all very dirty from such a busy day, and that did it for all the water we had hauled, except for a little bit for breakfast use. I stacked up the old tin cans on the trunks, took my bath, and went to bed too. The kids were all asleep as soon as their heads hit the pillows. That was only Thursday, our first full day all alone.

It was sort of like being on another planet or something. It was so quiet with no traffic, no other human beings, small rustlings in the grass; once in a while the dogs barked just for something to do, or at some passing scent in the breeze.

One of the things we brought up with us was a battery - powered radio, and we listened to it every time we were in the house. At 7 PM there was a program on KHAR called "Northwinds", which gave out messages to people living in the bush. Dixie had told us about the program; we had heard it once or twice in town and had wondered at some of the messages. That night, we got a message from Clyde saying a happy birthday to Bud, and telling me he got the door, and would bring it up Saturday on the train. Hooray!! What a relief. His message also said he missed us and loved us and would bring groceries, and he did get my note that I sent in with Dixie and Wally. He also said he was bringing the chain saw. That meant he could cut a bunch of wood for us. That would save us a lot of work. There was a little shed out back which leaned dangerously and would have to be torn down - it was supposed to be the woodshed, but of course it was empty.

Friday was much the same as Thursday; haul water, roll down weeds, find wood, and then it rained and got really chilly. So Friday evening I decided to light a fire in the sheepherders stove. It was a rusty old thing, but it was what the Rudders had used to heat with, so I put paper and kindling and a few boards in it and lit a fire. Got a nice roaring fire right away; but it started to fall out onto the floor through the holes in the sides and bottom. The heat just ate the rust up and we had one holey stove, with hunks of fire on the dry wood floor. Kept me busy with the metal dustpan; finally I got all the burning pieces of wood into the kitchen stove. Just to be sure, I poured some water on the dry floor in case there were any sparks I couldn't see.

Earlier, before it rained, the kids and I picked all the strawberries we could find to supplement our dwindling food supply. Shelley and I picked all the rhubarb and I cooked it with some sugar. While we were picking the rhubarb, Lisa and Debbie were playing and Debbie was eating highbush cranberries, which are very sour, and lots of strawberries. After dinner, when we managed to finish up all the food I had brought except for some pancake mix and a few staples, we had big bowls of strawberries for dessert.

Debbie woke up crying in the middle of the night, complaining that her tummy hurt, and proceeded to throw up all over the place. I never saw so many cranberries. She had just been swallowing them whole, and lots of strawberries too. After she got all of that out of her system, she was fine and went back to sleep while I cleaned up the mess. In the morning she was starved. I made her promise to stay away from the strawberry patch and all the cranberry bushes.

We had pancakes for breakfast. I made a few extra for munching until Clyde got off the train with some food. I hoped he was bringing lots of it, because I brought up what I though was enough for two weeks, and it only lasted four days! Hadn't counted on all this fresh air making us all so hungry. We just couldn't seem to get enough to eat.

The highlight of each day for the kids was when a train went by. They would run out or stop what they were doing to wave, and the engineer always blew the whistle and waved back, which gave them a big thrill. There seemed to be a freight train or two going by each day at different times.

We were all down at the tracks waiting for the passenger train when Clyde got off, and were we ever happy to see him! The kids didn't stop talking all the way to the house, telling him of all our fun adventures. He brought lots of food, and the chain saw, our good old ax, and other necessities of life, like a door to keep out the bears and the cold!

The first thing he did, while I fixed a meal, was to hang the new door, and it fit! Now I could move the trunks away from the doorway and get rid of the empty tin cans and not have to worry about a bear coming in through the holey old Army blanket, which we threw away. The door even had a window in it to let light into that end of the kitchen.

I asked Clyde to show me what I was doing wrong with the kitchen stove and to find out why it wouldn't get the oven hot enough to bake anything. He told me I was letting all the oven heat go out the chimney by not closing the damper!! I was a city girl, what did I know of 'dampers'? But I learned, and fast. When Clyde explained it, it made more sense, and I finally got it right. But it was also badly in need of cleaning; I had no idea you were supposed to take off the stovetop and scrape the soot off the top and down the sides and underneath the oven, which was packed with it. No wonder it wouldn't get hot enough to bake anything! Clyde inspected it all after we had cleaned it (what a dirty job) and discovered that there were holes at the back of the firebox, which he filled with furnace cement; he said it wasn't perfect, but it would have to do for a while. Later on, when I built the fire to cook supper, I burned the biscuits, the oven got so hot. So it was from one extreme to the other. I wondered if I would ever learn how to use it right? Like everything else in life, it took lots of practice, and over the next few days and weeks, I learned how.

We spent the rest of the day stacking the wood Clyde cut, and he threw away the little heating stove and the stovepipe, which was also full of holes, and fixed the window above our bed so it wouldn't fall out again if we wanted to open it, and checked the rest of the windows. He discovered that they were all loose, more or less. There were also many air leaks that would have to be fixed before it got cold. He would be bringing up a roll of plastic next time, he said, and our camp stove, so I wouldn't have to burn wood for every meal and could save some of the wood for heat in case it got cold before the barrel stove was shipped up and installed.

Clyde bringing in wood - Winter 1964-65

Oh how I hated to hear that Clyde had to work the next Saturday and wouldn't be able to come home. He was trying hard to get the trailer and truck sold, but until then he had to stay in town to support us all, except when he could get a Saturday off. He was impressed with all the work we had accomplished in such a short time and at how we had the house fixed up Of course he praised all the kids for helping me so much. It wasn't fancy, but at least it was clean and livable, even though the roof still did leak.

We made a huge list; some more lumber to enclose the sides of the roof, some more tar, stovepipe, nails and lumber for a woodshed, among numerous other things. Clyde knocked down the sagging shed; we didn't want it to fall on one of the kids. All he had to do was lean gently on one of the posts and it slowly crumpled to the ground. He thought we might be able to use the roof to put over the porch, which might keep snow away from the door. Also, the next time Clyde came home he was going to bring a big long chain for Johnnie and move him to a big stump south of the house, and Took would get Johnnie's old chain, and be on a stump to the north side, or the other way around, however it worked out. When the weather got damp, the smell of dog was too much right near the house. And besides, Clyde wanted to close in the bottom of the house to make it warmer for winter, so we would have to build two doghouses as well.

When the birthday cake I was baking for Bud was done, (I watched it like a hawk so it would not burn), we had a real party, complete with presents from both the Grandmas, and from us. The cake came out lopsided, but okay; the kids didn't mind a bit. Bud was pleased, and now that he is a man of eight, his next goal is a gun of his own. One of our gifts to him was his very own fishing rod and reel, which he had been wanting for a long time. But I don't think a gun will be forthcoming for a few years yet.

We spent the day Sunday stacking wood next to the back door; I don't know why we called it the BACK door, since it was the only door. And then we took both dogs and went for a walk, all of us, on the tracks with the gun, of course. The dogs seemed to get along fine by then. I thought that Johnnie finally realized that Took was still just a pup. We saw several black bears walking back and forth along the bank of the river and the kids were thrilled. They immediately wanted one for a pet! No thanks!

We asked the kids if they wanted to go back to town and they all yelled "NO!" They loved it out there, loved the freedom to make as much noise as they wanted to without having to worry about disturbing a neighbor; loved having so much space to run and play in, because since we had rolled down an immense area of weeds, they could play where the weeds were flattened, and not have to worry about getting lost, or eaten by a bear.

Everything was turning red and gold and beautiful. All the mountains were filled with color. Every window had a breath taking view. The only flaw was that Clyde had to stay in town for a while. We had a wonderful weekend, but it ended all too soon, and Clyde got on the train and went back to town. The kids and I were sad to see him go, and we had a quiet evening.

Time just flew, with all we had to do each day just to have water, heat, and food cooked. It was a lot more work than living in town with all the amenities, but that didn't seem to matter. What I missed most of all was hot and cold running water and a shower. Oh, a nice hot shower seemed the lap of luxury after a very short time. But we made do with the little round metal tub, which was all well and good for the kids, but I was too big for it, and if I sat in it like a real bathtub, my legs were outside of the tub. There was no way I would ever fit. But we managed to get clean after all.

I got mail from my folks and Clyde's folks, and was kept busy answering it and teaching the kids. Their schoolbooks came the second week we were there, and talk about busy! They arrived on the weekend train, the one weekend Clyde didn't come home because he had to work that Saturday. The train actually stopped and put off all the books and a box of food Clyde had sent up and all the mail.

The first week of school I was ready to tear my hair out by the roots, trying to figure out what I was supposed to do - in three different grades, all at once. Talk about frustrating! We arranged for the courses before moving up here, when we took the kids out of school in town. We had to get their records to send to Juneau, and when they came, the Correspondence Study courses all arrived at once. There was a big box of books and one of supplies for each child and manuals for each grade, for the home teacher. First grade, third grade and fourth grade. Once I stopped panicking and really sat down to read the directions it was plain enough; the kids seemed to like it just fine. So that Lisa wouldn't feel left out I had her do "school work" as well. She soon tired of it and found other things to play with. I really couldn't get much else done though.

The second time Clyde came up he put up a woodshed and each and every weekend he cut and hauled wood and filled it up so that we could keep warm and not have to work so hard. We often saw black bear, in fact almost every day there was one or two and one day a mama bear with two little cubs, they were so cute. But each one we saw was on the other side of the river (a good place for them to be). The kids were thrilled and actually, I was too. One night the dogs were barking and barking; it was dark and I couldn't see anything. The next day I looked around and found fresh bear tracks along the railroad tracks and on the path near a clump of cranberry bushes along the west boundary of our property. That's the closest a bear had come to the house since we'd been there, as far as I knew. But after the good hard frost we had, they all disappeared.

We saw fresh moose tracks crossing the railroad tracks and the dogs had been barking a lot, every evening about dusk and every morning there were fresh tracks about the same place for about a week. Must be a regular moose crossing there, or else one confused moose. Actually the Rudders told us that was where they crossed all winter. So we knew where to look to find the tracks. We were hoping that one would materialize in the flesh, so to speak, so that we could have some fresh meat.

We had been eating strawberries out of the patch nearly every day until we were getting tired of them and so I made some jam for later in winter out of what was left until the frost got them, finally. I think the weed cover probably kept the frost off of them

After we had been in our new home for several weeks, we met the foreman of Gold Creek section when he brought us our first batch of mail. His name was Louis Hammons and his crewman was Bill Thompson. They were both very nice men. Louis was married and promised to bring his wife Mabel to visit soon, and his three boys to play with our kids. What a treat that would be! Every couple of days they would stop by for coffee, and to see if the kids and I were okay, which relieved Clyde's mind of worry. Old Bill really took a shine to

Lisa. He called her his little blonde sweetheart; and called her 'Mona Lisa'. Of course he liked the other kids too, and they all liked him a lot, but Lisa especially. Bill was an old bachelor, crusty sourdough type, with a heart of gold.

The news was that the Anchorage to Fairbanks Highway was nearly complete; it would be called the Parks Highway. They only had to finish the bridge over the Big Susitna River north of the road turnoff to Talkeetna. It would probably be paved in the near future, one would hope, but most likely not until the summer, at least. And it would probably take several summers. The highway was about ten miles west of here, as the crow flies, over the big Susitna River and a mountain range or two.

It had been about five weeks; so far Clyde had been able to get home every weekend except the second one, and had our barrel stove set up with new stovepipe, and each evening we had a nice toasty fire in it, since it had been getting down to 30 degrees at night, and about 45 to 50 during the day. There was already snow on the top of the higher mountains.

Louis and Bill told us about a big pile of coal which was dumped down by the siding years ago when the old section house used to be across the tracks and they said there was probably some good lumps left and that we should go down with packsacks and sift around the pile to see if we could find any. Louis told us it would help with baking in the wood cookstove, and give better heat in the kitchen. So the next time Clyde came home, we all went down to the siding with old gunnysacks and pack boards and got a bunch of coal to burn. We had to search around to find it, because weeds had grown up all over the pile, and the lumps were few and far between until we dug down deep. Looked like there was quite a bit there, but it sure was dirty stuff, and seemed to get into everything.

I'd been washing clothes on a scrub board, which wasn't easy; the clothes didn't seem to get as clean as a washing machine, no matter how hard or long I scrubbed them. So I'd been sending the heaviest and dirtiest stuff to town with Clyde. The "gasoline washer" we inherited with this place was broken, of course. Wally had proudly proclaimed that they hadn't done any laundry for a whole year; that must be why, I guessed.

By that time I knew I was never cut out to be a teacher; how anyone could teach a class of thirty-to-forty kids all day long was really beyond me! One thing though; Bud was very good at arithmetic, and doing fine so far in spelling; but he needed a lot of help in phonics to speed up his reading. He was such an active little boy, he couldn't seem to sit still for more than two minutes at a time, didn't follow directions very well, was having difficulty learning cursive writing and was generally a problem. I imagine it must be even harder teaching your own kids. At least it was for me.

Debbie's work only took about one or two hours to get through each day, but Bud and Shelley's took three to four hours, sometimes more. Shelley read very well and with excellent understanding, so I didn't have to supervise much of her work. The subjects were Reading Arithmetic, Writing, Spelling, Science, Health, Social Studies, English and Art. That was a lot to get through in one day, each and every day. Debbie had less of course, being in first grade; Bud was in third grade, and Shelley in the fourth.

I loved it out here, the country was so beautiful and the air so fresh and clean, and the kids had a grand time running and yelling and making forts and climbing trees. There were about five acres around the house with the weeds rolled down or cut down in which the kids could run and play to their hearts' content. They kept the dogs with them and stayed within sight of the house; and Lisa stayed right with the older ones. After having been cooped up in that trailer court for over a year, it was like paradise to have so much room to run and play in.

I never realized how easy it was to get along without plumbing or electricity! The only really difficult thing so far was the laundry. That was a real chore, doing it by hand; the water in the creek was too cold, so it had to be heated some, even for rinsing, and that was a terrific amount of work.

Writing letters took up most of my evenings after the kids were asleep. I would write by kerosene lamp and most nights I was too tired to even read before falling asleep. The kids helped me with everything, mostly willingly; if they wanted to eat, I reminded them, they'd have to help me haul in wood, water and help with other chores each day - and they did love to eat!

I learned, in my "spare" time, how to bake bread in that cranky old woodstove oven; it really was easier to do it burning coal. It definitely took a lot of time and constant watching. I was looking forward to the time when my little propane apartment size stove with oven came up on the freight, so I wouldn't have to mess around with the old wood stove. It seemed like the kids ate it up faster than I could get it baked.

Around mid-September, the passenger train went on what was called the "winter schedule", which meant that there was no longer a daily passenger train, but only two a week. One going north to Fairbanks on Saturday and one going South to Anchorage on Sunday and one going north on Tuesday night, sometime in the middle of the night, and south on Wednesday, same time, about.

Then it snowed, our first snow on our homestead. It was Friday, October 16th, in the evening, and about four inches fell, and the sun came out about ten minutes before Clyde got off the train Saturday. We had a sunny weekend, and he went back on Sunday, and told two friends, Fred and Frank that the snow wasn't as deep here as it was in town, so they were going to come and pick out some property for Fred and his family, and Frank was going to help Fred get a cabin started. Then Betty, Fred's wife and their two kids would come up on the weekend train with Clyde. That sounded fine to me, but on Monday night it snowed again, and all day Tuesday until about midnight, when I finally went to bed. I felt certain that Fred and Frank wouldn't be coming with all that snow. I had no idea it hadn't snowed at all in Anchorage! And anyway, I reasoned with myself, I would surely hear the train if it did stop!

About 1:30 am I was wakened from a sound sleep by banging on the door! And there stood Fred and Frank, covered with snow, exhausted, and cold. The train had come and let them off about 12:30 am and they got off and just kept sinking down and sinking down clear up to their waists in the drifts that were so deep. What a surprise for them! It took them about an hour to plow through all that snow all the way to the house, in the dark. I fixed the couch into a bed for them, because there was no way they could possibly stay in the tent they had brought. They didn't even have a heater of any sort with them.

At least I had help for the rest of the week, as they couldn't start a cabin with so much snow on the ground. I was even able to get caught up on my washing and mending, and it was nice to have adult conversation.

The men weren't in the house all the time, of course; they went hunting every day, and looking for land too, but no wild animals were out and around. They took care of all the heavy chores, relieving me and the kids of them, so the kids got a lot of schoolwork caught up and we all had a good rest too, from the heavy work.

Then Friday night we were all listening to the Northwinds radio program after supper; the last message was from Clyde. It said: "To Mary, Shelley, Buddy, Debbie and Lisa at Sherman: At last, the GREAT DAY has arrived. I will be up Saturday, FOR GOOD!!!" Well, you never saw such a happy bunch - we screamed, yelled, shouted, cried and laughed, and Fred and Frank even joined in. I had thought the day would never come! And so we all had a party. I fixed cake and punch and we made snow ice cream, and had a great time; the kids got to stay up late and celebrate with us. It was such wonderful news for us. After seven and a half weeks mostly without their Dad and my husband, we were finally going to be a whole family again.

Saturday Clyde got off the train with a huge load of baggage, and Fred's wife Betty and their two kids. Of course none of them knew we had so much snow here, it hadn't snowed in town at all. We really had a house full; all crammed into our two little rooms. Betty was the first woman I had seen to talk to since moving up here, and I became hoarse from so much talking. I know her ears and Fred and Frank's also were ringing for at least a week afterward. I didn't know I could talk so much or so continuously. That was a long seven and a half weeks, mostly alone, but it was worth it.

Clyde had sold the trailer and the truck, paid off all our bills and quit his job. We had enough money to live on for the rest of the winter, and all the rest of our belongings were coming up on the freight the next week. Clyde had his application in to go to work for the railroad, and he hoped to be hired soon.

We had a great and fun weekend with our house full; the kids really enjoyed having those two kids to play with; Freddie and Tina were both near the ages of our two oldest. We had wall-to-wall beds, but were cozy and warm. Betty and Fred picked out the land they wanted to build their cabin on. They planned to come back in the spring to build and we would help them. Then, of course, when we got ready to build our log house they would help us. But first we had to clear the land and plant and all the rest of the requirements in order to get a deed to our property. They all went back to town on Sunday's train. It was snowing again, but not too cold; I could hardly believe Clyde was home to stay, at last! We were all so happy, and a complete family once again.

We discovered that there was a work crew parked at the railroad siding, when we went down there to dig for some coal. We had all gone down the tracks, pulling Lisa on a sled. As we passed the train cars, one of the men stuck his head out the door and yelled for us to come have some coffee, so we did. There were five train cars parked there, and a crew of ten linemen, repairing and replacing the railroad telephone lines; they told us they would be there for about ten days. When we told them we had come after more coal, they said they would haul it up to the house for us in the gas car, when next they went north, so we wouldn't have to drag it on the sled. They were all set up with a generator, running water, both hot and cold, just like in the city, and the works. We sacked up about 300 pounds of coal, loaded it on the gas car and walked back home. Later two men dropped it off and came up to the house for coffee. We enjoyed the visit, and a few days later, while I was fixing supper, the foreman of the gang stopped, came up to the house, and invited us to come see a movie at 6:30 pm at the siding. After we ate supper, we bundled up, pulled Lisa on the sled and the rest of us walked. They had a big movie projector and screen, and several large cans of film. The movie was a shoot-em-up western, called "The Violent Men", starring Glenn Ford and Barbara Stanwyck. We really enjoyed it. What a neat surprise that was, to go to a movie out in the middle of nowhere.

They were really nice men, all of them, and very friendly. They gave apples to all the kids, and cookies, gum and orange pop. All rare treats. Just before the movie started, the northbound freight stopped and dropped off a boxcar. It was full of our stuff, all 3700 pounds of it that Clyde had brought to the freight depot over the weeks to have shipped up here, including the aluminum room, some lumber, food, my gas cookstove (oh joy!) propane and kerosene, all the rest of the clothes, dishes, etc. that had been left in the trailer. The foreman said they would haul it all up to our house when they had time. What a blessing that was. I couldn't imagine hauling all that through nearly four feet of snow and many many trips for three quarters of a mile each trip. Of course we would use the dog, Johnnie, but we were so relieved we wouldn't have to do all that work ourselves! As it was, the work entailed just getting all that stuff hauled up to the house from the tracks, only about 100 yards, was quite a job, and we were certainly thankful we had not had to haul it farther.

Clyde fixed a dog harness out of several old broken ones, and harnessed Johnnie up to the hauling sled, which had also been broken, but Clyde repaired it as best he could and made it useable once more. The kids piled on for their first dogsled ride, and Johnnie pulled them to a stand of birch where Clyde was sawing up logs for the barrel stove. They enjoyed it so much they wanted to do it all day, but we told them they could only ride sometimes, that Johnnie would be all worn out otherwise. But oh, that dog did love to work in harness. He weighed about 110 pounds, was a beautiful light reddish-brown MacKenzie River husky, with black on his face and wolf's yellow slanted eyes. He loved the kids, and was a real clown of a dog. I hadn't tried to use him because he was stronger than I was and I didn't know how to put a harness on or anything, so we waited until Clyde was home. Johnnie pulled a load of about 300 pounds of wood home, while the kids, Clyde and I walked back, from the woodpile. Just before we got back to the house, the harness broke. But we had parts of six harnesses and some old snowshoes the Rudders had left there, all needing extensive repair. We worked on them all winter, until we had several good harnesses and one good pair of snowshoes, or at least useable ones.

By that time we had received about three letters from Dixie. She said they were enjoying their new home, canning vegetables and fruit; Wally was feeling much better in the warmer climate, and Dixie loved the running water, electricity and appliances in her new home. Before it snowed, and after the hard frost, I had dug up some flower roots she had marked and sent them to her.

We got lots of mail - Louis brought it whenever it came and he got down our way. He and Bill usually stopped in for coffee and whatever I had baked that day, usually cookies, or a pie or just bread and jam.

What nice men they were down at the switch. On Halloween night they came up to our house, and brought apples, oranges, and candy for the kids. What a treat for them, especially the oranges. They told the kids they had played a trick on them and brought them some treats so they wouldn't have to go trick or treating in the deep snow. The kids all thought they were funny. Those nice guys had been helping Clyde haul up coal and wood whenever they weren't working, and they had really made things easier for us.

Clyde was able to put up shelves in the kitchen and made storage space in the bedroom as well. It took a lot of work to get started on a homestead, more than we had ever thought. But we gradually got things accomplished. There just wasn't enough time in the day; we got up at 7:00 am, and kept going all day long until 10:00 pm, when we collapsed into bed. There was no end to the work, it seemed. We continued to struggle along with schoolwork, and all went well until someone stopped by for coffee or one of the dogs got loose, or any other excuse for a 'break'. We had more 'recesses' than any real school!

We saw a grand total of three movies while the line crew was parked on the switch. They were there longer than they thought they would be, and the other two movies we were invited to see were one with John Wayne, and Barry Fitzgerald and Maureen O'Hara - an unbeatable combination. It took place in Ireland and was very funny. The last one was a western, with Fred MacMurray and a Mr. Magoo cartoon. We enjoyed them all, especially the kids. The crew had fresh apples and oranges for the kids each time, which was a real treat in this country in those days and hard to get unless you lived in town and had an unusually large food budget in the winter. They were so expensive, and would freeze if we ordered them up by freight. The line crew finished their work on the telephone lines and moved on. We missed them a lot, a nice bunch of guys.

Louis and Bill from Gold Creek helped us out a lot as well. They said if we didn't have a lot of wood here at the house and lots of coal, we would most likely freeze to death because, they said, it got awfully cold here and this drafty old cabin took a lot of wood to keep it warm.

But the weather had been sort of warm; we had a mild blizzard, when over a foot of new snow fell on top of the old. It was 30 to 32 degrees most of the time for that few days and before that it was 10 degrees during the day and zero to 2 above at night. Clyde would fill the barrel stove as full as he could get it, and load the kitchen stove with coal, and every two hours or so he had to get up and put more wood in the barrel stove.

We found out from Louis and Bill that we were burning the wrong kind of wood. Clyde had been cutting out the old dead and half-dead cottonwoods from the grove directly behind the house, and also birch from a patch of trees about a quarter of a mile south of the house. The cottonwood burned up like paper or wouldn't burn at all, and put out very little heat; birch burned very hot, but was all green wood, and hard to get started. So the woodshed was mostly full of cottonwood, with some green birch mixed in.

Clyde, Shelley and Bud, and sometimes I would take the sled out to the woods and haul back wood, or we would go to the siding and haul back coal. After Louis and Bill told us what we should be cutting, - dead birch and dead spruce to use as kindling, - we were doing better, but it was still a lot of work to keep the house warm. We had quite an impressive stack piled up in and around the shed, and cords of wood next to the house. It was fun to work the dog - we only used Johnnie, since Took didn't have sense enough to learn how to pull a sled. We tried him hooked on behind Johnnie; he was run over twice, dragged a few feet, and wouldn't even try to get up. We also tried many other ways, but Took just wasn't smart enough to learn, or perhaps he was too smart, and just lazy. He ate as much as Johnnie, even though he was smaller, but we knew he wasn't full-grown yet. Johnnie looked like an overgrown teddy bear with his winter coat all fuzzy; the kids nicknamed him 'Teddy Bear'. He certainly was an eager worker. When he saw the harness, he wanted to go, right now!

In my so-called 'spare time', I'd been knitting thick mittens for all the kids out of polar yarn and also making curtains for the bedroom, writing letters, helping Clyde with necessary repairs to snowshoes, dog harness, dog sled and other things that seemed to need constant attention or repair in some way.

We received Northwinds messages from time to time from family from Outside, (Lower 48) who all seemed to think we were 'deprived' in some way, letting us know they had mailed a box to us.

Another "care package" as we called them. It was neat getting those packages, with all the things we didn't buy here, like Sugar Frosted Flakes, Rice a Roni dinners, candy, gum, packages of Kool-Aid, cake mixes, what my mother thought were necessities of life! They were always welcome, and a real treat.

We met a lineman from Talkeetna one day, when he stopped in for coffee and to warm up. His name was Tony Wolfe, and he told us all the news of the "Outside world". It seems that, even though we were told differently before, the Anchorage to Fairbanks highway, which would be called the "Parks Highway" when completed, was only half done. It went a little north of the Talkeetna cutoff, Tony said, and from the Fairbanks end it was completed to a little south of Healy, so far all gravel and rock. It was rerouted from the original plan, Tony said, and it would be directly across the mountain range and river from us, about ten miles as the crow flies.

That was around mid-November of our first winter on the homestead, and by that time we'd had a couple of visits from Louis' wife Mabel and their boys; I liked Mabel so much - what a neat lady she was! She was Eskimo, and we seemed to hit it off right away. The boys were ages, two, three and four and Debbie and Lisa had lots of fun playing with them. Even our older two seemed to enjoy them a lot. Mabel was planning to come down from Gold Creek and spend the whole day with me in the near future, she said. She wanted me to help her understand the pattern she bought at the Knit Shop in Spenard, where I learned to knit. She had never worked with six colors of yarn before and a friend in the trailer court taught me how, so I would attempt to teach Mabel if I could still remember. I looked forward to the day. School would be dismissed, joyfully!

Talkeetna, mid- 1960's

A few days later more "care packages" came from my folks containing books, magazines, yarn, Dr. Seuss books for the kids, and a 'Dinner on Us' box with Rice a Roni mixes, cake mixes, dry cereal, cans of meat and tuna and a note that a box of apples would be sent soon, by faster mail. One box was from Aunt Ida, my mom's youngest sister, with warm hats, mittens and mufflers for all of us. How nice that was. We could never have too many, since we seemed to have wet mittens and so forth hanging up over the stoves to dry all the time. She also sent warm sweaters and a beautiful black knit suit, which just happened to be the right size for Mabel. I was sure Mabel would love it; it was so soft and warm.

When Mom's box of apples arrived, Louis dropped it off and it was two degrees below zero. I was so afraid the apples would all be frozen, but when we got the box opened, my mom had packed the apples so well, surrounded by sponges, they were all in excellent shape. What a treat to have fresh fruit in the middle of winter! We certainly enjoyed them, every one.

Most of the time we got our groceries from Teeland's Country Store in Wasilla. All we had to do was mail them a list of what we needed, and they would fill that list and put it on the northbound freight train, the one that stopped to deliver freight to homesteaders once a week. The freight charge was $4.00 per hundred pounds. The Teeland's would put the bill in one of the boxes and we would send cash back to them by return mail. If we didn't have enough change to come up with the exact amount, we would usually send more, and the Teeland's would apply it as credit to future orders. It was a joy to do business with them. They always filled our orders promptly and fully. If they were out of a specific item, they would substitute with the closest they had. And they always sent suckers or loose candy or some other treat, for each of the kids. And at Christmas time, they sent a box of chocolate covered cherries and a calendar for Clyde and me and many items of fun things for the children, as well as Christmas candy. We really missed them so much when they sold their business.

The freight, commonly called "The Peddler", came by Tuesday nights, heading north, and dropped flares at our path, by the mailbox, which we had put up approximately 30 feet from the tracks so the snowplow blades wouldn't hit it, and when the box car with our stuff in it came along side the flares, it stopped and the trainmen unloaded the freight, then went on. We stacked the boxes on the toboggan and pulled it to the house.

By that time, most of the train crews knew us, or had met us, some of the trains would go by and toss off a newspaper or some magazines, and usually candy for the kids. Of course the kids would all run out to wave at every train during the day. Sometimes even in bare feet in the snow! Of course the trainmen always blew the whistle for the kids too. It was a high point of each day, and also another chance to take a break from schoolwork.

Around mid-November, we saw the sun no more. It would just sort of slither around, just under the tops of the mountains at the south end of our valley, shedding its dimmed light for about three or four hours, then it was dark again. Sometimes the moon shining on the snow made the nights brighter than some days. This lasted until mid-January, when we would once again get a brief but welcome glance of the sun, unless it was a cloudy day, and longer each day until the summer solstice in June, when the process would be reversed once again.

The first week of December I took the train to town and took Lisa with me. Betty and Fred met us at the station and we spent the next two days with them. I had to buy another ax, sledgehammer and splitting wedge for Clyde, do some grocery shopping and Christmas shopping. I enjoyed visiting with Betty and a few other friends we hadn't seen for awhile. I mailed canned salmon to everyone in our families in the States and hoped it all got there without any damage. It was 40 degrees below zero when we got back home on the middle of the night train Tuesday night. BRRR! Northern lights were out in full force. They were beautiful.

We didn't get a moose that late season, but Bill brought us a leg from the one he shot. He said he wouldn't ever use up a whole moose by himself. The leg was hung in the back porch. Clyde shot a few ptarmigan as well, and we had plenty of meat in our 'freeze box' outside.

We managed, just, to keep warm in our little cabin with both stoves going full blast. We all had long underwear, which we slept in, and we had to put plastic sheeting up on all the windows, because the drafts were simply awful. When the wind blew, it came in all around the ill-fitting windows and made ice form on the glass on the inside. The plastic helped, but there were still air leaks all over. As long as the wind did not blow, the cold was bearable.

I don't know how we ever thought we would have been able to put up a shelter for the winter! What Cheechakos we were! We never would have made it without that old shack to start out in. There simply hadn't been enough time from September 8th until it snowed to get anything built! Much less firewood cut for heat or any of the rest of it. The only insulation in that old shack was a layer of plastic between the outside wall and the inside wall. But back in 1964 insulation was only 2½ inches thick; even that would have been a huge improvement.

Mabel came for the day as promised, shortly after Lisa and I got back from town, and after the weather warmed up to about 10 degrees above. Lisa had caught cold while we were in town, but was over it in just a few days, and the other kids did not catch it. We enjoyed the visit tremendously, and I was able to help Mabel with her sweater, which was beautiful; white background with red and pink roses contrasted with the deep green leaves, done in thick Canadian wool. There was a large and medium rose on the back and small roses on the pockets, with varied shades of green leaves. It was lovely when it was finished. Louis also brought us a front leg of their moose, and so we had a front and back leg besides some the train hit down by Curry the week before. By that time it looked like a butcher shop around there.

Betty and Fred and family weren't able to come up for Christmas as they had planned, but they sent up a cute little seven week old kitten for the kids, which they promptly named 'Sam-I-Am" after a Dr. Seuss character. He was gray and white tiger striped with blue eyes, half Siamese and half alley cat, and a playful little devil.

Our first Christmas on our little homestead was wonderful. With the few gifts we were able to buy or make for the kids, and Aunt Ida and Grandma sent five boxes of things; Mom and Dad sent boxes of gifts for us all. They all arrived in plenty of time for Christmas, so we had a large pile of presents under the tree, instead of just a few, and a nice big orange and apple in each kids' stocking.

Clyde and the three oldest kids went out into the woods Christmas eve, and found a perfectly beautiful little tree, about four feet tall; Clyde made a stand for it, and all the kids - even Lisa- decorated it with home made paper chains, our old decorations, and a lovely manger scene my mom sent; it turned out to be a really pretty tree. We had frosted cookies to hang on it, in different shapes and colors, and candy canes. We put Christmas cards up all over the walls and strung them all around the windows, and were very festive. We even got a nice Northwinds message on Christmas eve from my family in California, which made us feel as if we were closer to them, wishing us all a 'Merry Christmas and a happy holiday season.'

Louis and Mabel and their boys came down from Gold Creek on Christmas day and brought apples, oranges, nuts and three frying chickens and a game of checkers. And the beautiful sweater that Mabel gave up on and begged me to finish for her. We had a nice visit and our kids had presents for their three boys; everybody had a good time. I had some fudge and frosted date ball cookies and a few other homemade things wrapped and ready for Mabel and Louis, who had become such very good friends in such a short time. They were both really great people.

For Christmas dinner I fixed a canned ham with pineapple glaze, some canned corn on the cob, which I found while in Anchorage, sweet potatoes, fresh hot rolls, ptarmigan stuffed with dressing, and pumpkin pie. There were no leftovers.

Shelley made up a little play all by herself, using dolls as Mary, Joseph, and baby Jesus, and the three of our kids entertained all of us by singing a few carols for us. In between, Shelley read the story of the first Christmas. It was really something - a total surprise for us. We knew they had been cooking up something, but we had no idea it was so elaborate. Shelley was really an inventive child. We hated to see the Hammons leave; we all enjoyed them so much. I told Mabel I would do my best to finish the sweater, but had little time, so I hoped she didn't expect it too soon. Her answer was, "whenever".

The train crews threw off Christmas stockings filled with candy and treats for the kids as the train went by on Christmas Eve. We had a wonderful time on our first Christmas in our new home in the wilderness.

My mother sent out a newsletter with her Christmas cards that first year, and her list was always long. I heard from about 40 people, some of whom I did not know. In Mom's newsletter, she included the news about our living through the Big Earthquake, and then about our homesteading land and living in the wilderness, telling everyone that we were the sole inhabitants of the "little town called Sherman, Alaska, population six." And so I heard from many people, and endeavored to answer all their questions to the best of my ability, starting with people I knew, of course and then my correspondence kept growing by leaps and bounds. But we loved to get mail. It took me well into January, nearly the end of the month, to get all the original letters answered.

The kitten, poor little Sam I Am, died of a mysterious ailment. He just began to wail and couldn't seem to get up and it was no use; whatever we did to try to help him, it was obvious he was in excruciating pain and there was nothing to be done but to put him out of his misery. It was very strange, he was fine, playing with a string and happy, and then all of a sudden he couldn't walk or breathe, and so he went to kitty heaven. We all missed him; he was such a playful and cute little clown of a kitten. And of course the children all cried.

The next day or very soon after that sad event, we got a letter from a woman in Talkeetna who heard we were looking for another sled dog or two to enlarge our 'one-dog-team'. She said she had a female puppy we could have if we wanted to come and get it. So Clyde got a ride into Talkeetna on one of the railroad gangs' gas car, and came home the next day on the passenger train with not one, but FOUR of the most adorable white Siberian Husky pups- two females and two males. The lady gave the females to Clyde and sold him the males for $10 each. She needed the money pretty badly, as her husband's trap lines hadn't done so well that year.

Lisa & Shelley with Copper

The kids each picked the puppy they liked best and named each one after a place in Alaska. Lisa's puppy had pale blue eyes, a rare and very pretty combination. His name was Tanana, or Tanny for short; he had pale tan coloring on his back and ears; the rest of him was white. Debbie's pup was all white with a few scattered black hairs on her rump; her name was Chena. Buddy's pup had the prettiest markings; his name was Copper. He had scatterings of tan and black and red on his back mixed with white and a white blaze between his eyes, dark ears and top of head, and the rest of him was white. He was so scared after getting off the train that he hid behind the couch for half a day. Shelley's pup was all white; a wee bit smaller than the other three, and had pale tan behind her ears. Her name was Crystal, or Crissy for short. They were the cutest and fluffiest little things, weighing about 20 pounds apiece, with very large feet. We knew they would be huge, at least as big as Johnnie.

Lisa & Copper

Johnnie was quite jealous of the puppies when Clyde first brought them home, and growled at them. But almost at once he decided to adopt them and worried over them like a mother hen. It was really fun to watch them together. We built a 12 by 12 foot pen with a house for the pups to sleep in, and they all slept in a heap, piled on top of each other. They had been born outside and were used to the cold, and really didn't like it inside. It was too warm for them. Johnnie of course was tied to his doghouse on a long chain. We let them all loose to run each day for a short time. Johnnie let them climb all over him and chew on his ears and tail, and when they began to wander he would herd them back towards the house. The wolves kept prowling by the river at night; we would hear them howl, and Johnnie would answer them. What a mournful and eerie sound the wolf's howl is!

We had to constantly reinforce the puppy's pen. They grew so fast, and began to climb out. Johnnie would bark frantically whenever one of them got loose, so we always knew. We used whatever was at hand to reinforce the pen, originally put up of spruce and birch poles, and then reinforced with aluminum panels, snowshoes, anything else on hand to keep them in. They were so cute and fun to watch - they would bound in and out of snowdrifts, disappearing completely from time to time, and scramble right out again. It was harder than ever to get any schoolwork done then.

Bud and Johnnie on a stump   **Bud & Lisa with Copper**

After about a month, they were pretty well used to their collars and leashes, and followed along when they were being walked and mostly came to their names when called. We got them used to a harness later on, and hitched them up, one at a time to a light sled to get them used to pulling weight. The only pup not responding to pulling was Tanny, the blue eyed one. He simply would not pull.

Johnnie taught them how to howl. It was a riot to watch. He would get them all to sit in a circle around him, (more or less,) and he would put his muzzle in the air and howl long and low. Then he would look at all of them as if to say, "Now you try it." They would have their little heads cocked to the side listening, and actually put their little muzzles up in the air and yip and whine. Johnnie kept it up until they came out with something that passed for a howl. Soon they were howling for meals, or when the train whistled, when the wolves howled, any time at all. They did very well, except for poor little Copper. That poor pup sounded like he was in great pain when he tried to howl; he would let loose with sort of a hoarse moan, like a sick cow. But he did try, and certainly did have a distinctive voice. It never really improved throughout his entire life.

Mary, Clyde & Lisa with Johnnie

When the pups howled for meals, Johnnie did too. When we let the pups loose for a run, they always headed straight for Johnnie. We couldn't let Took loose because he ran away every time, and we had the very dickens of a time getting him back. The pups didn't have much to do with him either; he seemed to be a loner. We usually let Johnnie loose with the pups because they liked to roam far a field, and he kept them herded close to the house. It worked out beautifully.

One weekend in late January Fred came up and he and Clyde went hunting ptarmigan. They came upon a trail of blood on the railroad tracks, which led into the woods. Clyde had a pair of snowshoes strapped on his back, so he followed the trail of blood into the woods. He hadn't gone far when he saw the moose struggling to get up; so Clyde shot it, since it was obviously wounded anyway. He sent Fred back to the house to get me and the dogsled, and Fred didn't feel like going back, so he stayed with the girls while Buddy and I went with Johnnie pulling us on the sled. Clyde had the only pair of serviceable snowshoes. We brought the ax along and some butcher knives, and it was the closest I had ever been to a moose. Are they ever big!! I must say, if you had never ridden on hard packed snow on a dogsled for over a mile, then plowed through six feet of soft dry snow, sinking every other step to your waist for about an eighth of a mile into the woods, wrestled for hours pulling and tugging on an 1,100 pound dead bull moose in the same soft snow so you could gut and skin it, and come home covered from head to foot with frozen blood, you just haven't lived! In 5 degree below zero weather, too!

When Buddy and I got there, Clyde had it about half gutted, but needed help turning and shifting it, it was so big. So I helped him, and Buddy stayed near Johnnie and the sled. It took us three or four hours just to gut it and chop it into quarters; by that time it was getting dark, so we only brought one hindquarter home - about 250 pounds, we estimated, leaving the rest until the next day. Believe me, it was a job, hauling that out in the sled over deadfalls, ditches, stumps and what all, but good old Johnnie worked hard. And with much pushing, pulling and tugging, we all managed.

We had no idea it was such hard work to gut and quarter a moose. There must have been a quicker and easier way to do it, and eventually we found out there was. But that first one was a real challenge. Also, like anything else, it takes practice. This moose had been hit by a train, and had a broken leg, with the bone sticking through, and had dragged itself off the tracks to the spot where Clyde found it. We were afraid the wolves would get the rest of the meat before we got to it the next morning, but there were no tracks the next day at all, and Clyde got the rest out and home, a quarter at a time. It took him most of the day, and Fred helped him with some of it. The only place Clyde didn't get bloody was his beard, and that was covered with ice. What a sight!

We thought there was about seven or eight hundred pounds of meat hanging in the shed aging and we sent some of the meat home with Fred, whatever he had room for. By that time we had used up most of the meat we got from Louis and Bill, so that was like a gift from God.

The kids surely were good. They all pitched in and brought in wood every day, even little Lisa. She would bring in a little chunk of wood and yell, "Hebby, momma, hebby." She would throw it on the floor and go out for more. I thought if I could only get her to put it in the wood box, that would be great. But she was only two, and I hoped she would improve with time. She was such a sweetie. All the kids got the wood in, and filled up the wood boxes as fast as they could so they could let the dogs loose and play. They loved it, no matter how cold it was, except when it was 40 degrees below zero, and we wouldn't let them go out when it was that cold. No chores or play outdoors when it was possible to freeze your lungs!

We had to chop ice out of the creek and melt it for our drinking water by that time, and there was always a tub of snow on both stoves melting for dishwater, laundry, baths, etc. It was a lot of work, just to try to keep clean. We really had taken modern conveniences for granted until we no longer had them. I certainly missed a hot shower!!!

By that time, we had about 16 weeks of school behind us, and Debbie was able to read, and loved school. She had always been such a scatterbrain; she surprised me how well she had done. Guess her active little mind needed to be schooled. She was really eager to learn. Bud and Shelley were doing well also, but their teacher was worn out at the end of each day. School surely took a lot of time and effort. It was like beginning in grade one for me, all over again. Of course by that time there was so much more for the children to learn than there had been when I was in first grade.

Winter was a beautiful time of year on the homestead, especially when there was a full moon. It would be almost brighter outside than during the day, like a fairyland, all sparkling with diamonds. It was a dry sort of cold, and we didn't seem to feel it as much as we had in Missouri, where the humidity was always so high. We banked both fires every night, closed the dampers, left the drafts open a hair or two, and both stoves were piled full; they usually held the fire all night, since we were burning the right kind of wood, finally. One of us woke up about 2:00 or 3:00 am to check the fires and throw on another log or two. We were managing to keep cozy and warm in spite of that drafty old house.

We had a solid week of snowfall, another four feet of it. The deeper the snow got, the more moose the trains hit, and we had quite a bit of meat hanging in the shed by that time. Whatever wasn't fit for human consumption went to the dogs. I had to can some of it because there was way too much meat to eat before spring thaw, and we didn't want any of it to spoil. It was too much work hauling it to the house, and the meat was too good to waste.

We saw many displays of northern lights, all different and beautiful. It seemed to me that the lights were out when it got colder, or else it got colder after a display of lights. But something changed each time. Then it got warm, 35 to 40 degrees and the weather was varied; snow melting, raining, snow mixed with sleet, more snow, generally bothersome weather all around.

As the meat thawed, I canned it, and brined it and salted it. In the midst of all that, my pressure cooker sprang a leak and we had to order another one. Meanwhile, Mabel loaned me her canner so I could get on with the job. When my new pressure canner came on the freight, the train day, which was Saturday, Lisa and I took the train up to Gold Creek and returned Mabel's canner to her. It cost 30 cents one way.

I met our other neighbors, Mr. and Mrs. Erickson and their two teen-age daughters. They lived on their homestead behind the section house. All these people were there to meet the train, hoping to get mail or meet passengers. There was also an Athabaskan Indian woman named Nellie Callahan, who had a homestead about a mile from the section house where Mabel and Louis lived. Nellie's husband John owned the gold mine there at Gold Creek. It was nice to get away from home for a few hours and talk to other people. Mabel and I had a great visit. She wouldn't let us go home until she fed us supper.

Louis stopped by midweek, and said the Tuesday night passenger train hit and killed a moose on the Sherman siding, and if we wanted it for the dogs, it was there. He said it probably wasn't much good for anything else but dog food. So Clyde went down and skinned it out and brought home the front and hindquarters, but left most of the rib cage after cutting off the meat, as it was pretty badly bruised and torn up. We knew if the weather continued to be so warm we would have to dry and smoke all of that meat for the dogs. However, it should keep for another three to four weeks since the meat hadn't aged yet.

We'd seen at least a dozen moose just wandering around aimlessly. Poor things, the snow was so deep and so hard for them to maneuver in, that's why they stuck close to the tracks where the going was easier for them. And that's why so many were hit by the trains.

We varied our diet of moose meat with ptarmigan; Clyde had good luck keeping us supplied. Meanwhile, I had finished Mabel's sweater, and she came down to get it and we visited some more. It only took me three months to finish it, working on it in my "spare time" when I wasn't canning, cooking, teaching, butchering, what a busy life!!

It was about mid-March, and Clyde decided he would dig a well under the house, in the "cellar", which was only a depression under the house, and not really deep enough to work as a true cellar. But there was a trap door in the floor leading down to it, so Clyde dug away, and hauled buckets of dirt out and scattered them on the paths outside to help melt the snow faster. He had no idea whether he would hit water or not, but the cellar needed to be dug out anyway since it was unusable as it was.

He hit a big rock the size of the house about eight feet down, so we had a cellar eventually at least. We needed it for storing potatoes and other vegetables, as well as canned goods. We thought it would be nice to have running water in the house besides through the roof! Alas, it was not meant to be.

The creek opened up just after mid-March so we didn't have to chop ice for drinking water any more. But the snow was rotting underneath and that made it practically impossible to go anywhere, even on paths, without sinking suddenly clear to the waist.

There was an owl in the grove of cottonwoods behind the house, hooting at us every evening, and some camp robbers, (some people called them moose birds), around in the yard.

It turned colder right after I finished canning and salting all the moose meat, making the snow hard as a rock, and walking and sledding was better than it had been all winter. Clyde and Buddy went across the frozen Susitna River to explore an old trapper's cabin. They followed fresh moose tracks across, reasoning that if the ice would hold a moose, it would hold them. They were right, and made it safely across, and back again. The old trapper's cabin had been unused for fifteen or twenty years by that time, except by occasional bears. The roof was partially collapsed, and I suppose by now there is no sign it ever was there. For a few days we were able to explore lots of the back areas of our property, and found moose tracks everywhere. That time, the creek stayed open for only three days then froze over solid again, and so we were back to ice chopping once more.

Chapter 11 Springtime at Last!

B y the end of March, we had had over a week of 40 to 60 degree weather, and we were positive it was spring. The creek was running again and the Susitna River had opened in the middle.

The snow level melted down to about two and a half feet, and then it started snowing again. It came down hard and heavy, and we knew spring was finished once again. We wondered if we would ever see the ground again, it had been so long.

I packed up the three oldest kids and went to Anchorage. They had six month's allowance saved up to spend, and had been doing good work in school, so they got their promised trip to town, and all of us had a fine time. We did get to see the ground again; from Wasilla to Anchorage there was no snow!! The ground looked strange after all the months of unrelieved white at home. We went to church, saw a movie, stocked up on blue jeans, shoes and underwear for all, ran some errands, visited some friends and came home thoroughly worn out, all of us.

We stayed with Betty and Fred again; they planned to come up the day before Easter, moving up, actually, snow or no snow, they said. So Clyde went to Anchorage the Thursday before Easter to help Fred move all his things to the freight depot. When he got off the train Saturday, Betty and Fred, Tina and Freddie, two dogs and two cats were with him.

Louis and Mabel and their boys came down from Gold Creek for the fun and stayed for dinner. I fixed an eight pound boneless ham, sweet potatoes, deviled eggs, three pumpkin pies, canned corn on the cob, mashed potatoes, and ham gravy, peas, homemade bread and the works. We hadn't had such a feast since Christmas, and a good time was had by all. All of the kids had an Easter egg hunt together.

Betty and Fred and kids stayed with us for a few days until their furniture and household goods arrived on the Tuesday freight following, then we helped them move into their insulated tent the next day, fixed up to accommodate a woodstove. It was nice to have a neighbor ¾ of a mile away, but that was close enough for me. Clyde went down each morning to help Fred cut trees down, cut them into twenty foot lengths and notch them. Soon they started building their cabin.

There had been a pack of pretty, bushy-tailed fox running around an acre or two behind the house, and we were able to catch a glimpse of them now and then. Whenever the fox were near, the dogs would bark like crazy, until the fox left the area. They seemed to know they weren't in any danger from the dogs, though. Then they moved on.

We were all happy to be back home, and best of all, none of us picked up any germs from town to spoil our near-perfect health record for the winter. That was the first trip to town for the three oldest kids since we moved there seven months before.

The bears were out south of us, and we knew they would be here soon. Old-timers said that you can smoke the hams and rib meat, and use it like bacon. They said you can't tell it from pork, and it has to be cooked like pork, well done. Bears, it seems, are of the pork family. Also, and I can say this from experience, there is no better shortening than rendered bear fat for pastries or anything. I didn't believe it at the time, but found out later that it was true. Properly rendered bear fat made the fluffiest biscuits, and the flakiest pie crusts I had ever baked.

The pups had grown and grown, they weighed nearly 50 pounds each, and the time had come to hitch them to the big sled with Johnnie. They all did fine, except for Tanny. But they all mostly wanted to play. We took them, one at a time, and led them around pulling the sled; that worked well. They all seemed to get the idea. Tanny and Took were the only failures, and we decided then that we would have to get other homes for them.

At that time our diet consisted of canned moose, Spam, salted dried moose and plenty of beans and cornbread, canned vegetables, but no fresh meat. We were waiting for the bears to come out of hibernation. One old bear came out at Curry, but he was sort of a pet, they said. The cook fed him pies. He hung around there for handouts every summer. They called him "Georgie". Some of the men on the freight crews didn't appreciate having a bear in the way when they stopped there for dinner, and one of them, we heard, put snuff in the Bear's pie and poor old Georgie was never seen there again!

Only eight more weeks of school remained until summer break and we had quite a stock of seed and were planning to plant 150 pounds of seed potatoes, also peas, radishes, spinach, turnips, lettuce, beets, carrots, onions, green beans, and sweet potatoes. We found out later that sweet potatoes did not grow here because the growing season was too short and cool, and also green beans did not do well for the same reasons.

Clyde and Fred were going to town the first week of June to work and they would stay in Fred's trailer, so they had to get Fred's cabin built by then.

I had a .45 pistol, which I had learned how to use, and I wore it in a holster wherever I went outside of the house, because it was more convenient and lighter to pack around than the heavy old 30.06 rifle. I was teased by our new neighbors about being the "Annie Oakley of Sherman, Alaska." Clyde wanted me to get a .44 magnum because, he said, a .45 may not be a big enough gun to actually stop a bear if I had to; meanwhile I was counting on the noise factor.

It was finally May, and there was still a foot of snow on the ground. We hoped it would be gone by the end of the month, at least. It melted some each day when the sun was out or when it wasn't snowing, but the snow that fell didn't stick, by then.

We decided that we definitely needed a cat, because the shrews, tiny destructive mice, got in the house easily and were such nasty dirty things. We had all our dry food in metal cans so no mice could get to it. But they got on whatever surfaces there were and messed all over the place. Betty's cat, little Sam-I-Am's mother, had just had kittens again, three of them, and we decided to take them, all. Our kids wanted to name them Ding, Dong, and Belle. Ding and Dong were males, of course - one was black, the other tiger striped, and Belle was gray and white. Clyde and I thought one cat would be enough, but the kids couldn't stand to think of Fred drowning the other two, and no one could decide which one to take, so we would end up with all three kittens. Fred wanted to take Took as a watchdog, so they would have one on each side of the tent. Their other dog was a very old little Chihuahua, strictly a house pet, and a more unlikely animal to have in the bush than I can think of.

It was late in May, and several things happened, it seemed, all at once. First of all, Took got loose and got into the tent, and ate the three kittens, and Fred shot Took, and that took care of Took, poor useless unlovable dog. They still had Pal for a watchdog, and the same old toothless going blind Chihuahua they called "Mighty Mite", and their mama cat.

Our neighbors certainly didn't last long. They stayed exactly three weeks in their tent. Clyde and Fred worked every day on their cabin, and they got all four walls up, the windows in and the doorjambs in place. Then Fred was called back to town to work for the summer, and Betty didn't want to stay out here without Fred, so she decided to go back to town and work too. They planned to be back up to put on the roof, doors and floor, whenever Fred got a weekend off. We all hoped the bears wouldn't get into the tent, which was full of furniture, canned goods, and other belongings.

We worked on the garden, getting it ready to plow and plant in about two weeks. It was certainly noisy at that time. The ice had been coming down the Susitna River in big chunks, - grinding, crashing and banging away as it went. There definitely was a lot of ice, and the roar and crash went on day and night, not that there was any night, as such, by that time. It was daylight all the time by then and we had put the darkest drapes back on the windows so that we could sleep.

The ducks and geese were back, but we hadn't seen any bear so far. The river made enough noise to wake up any bear, though.

Clyde was building a room on the house. We had been peeling logs and he had ripped large boards from cottonwood trees with the chainsaw. The room Clyde was building was entirely home made, with six inch logs (peeled) for rafters, frame, floor joists, and so on, and eighteen inch logs for the foundation. The walls were of ripped boards, from large cottonwood logs, rather rough; we wish we had a sawmill, but had to do with what we had. The room started out to be a storage area and workroom, but eventually became our bedroom.

Clyde planned to go to town June 1st to go to work, if everything worked out that way, which meant the kids and I would be alone again all summer, except for weekends, unless Mom Lovel came up to spend the summer. We wrote letters back and forth all winter, and she had been thinking it over and we did our best to convince her to come. Clyde's mom loved the outdoors, and we just knew she would love it up here if she ever did come.

We had only five weeks of school to go - I certainly needed the rest.

In our spare time, we raked and chopped roots out of the garden site. By that time nearly all the snow was gone around the house and yard, but there were still patches a foot deep here and there. The sun 'set' about 10:30 pm, and it was dusky-light outside until it rose again about 1:30 am. Before long we would have sun until nearly midnight, and sunrise about an hour later.

A moose walked slowly up the tracks heading north one day in late May, while we were eating lunch. It was a big bull, and he stopped opposite the house to stare at us awhile. We were all looking out the window thinking what nice juicy steaks he would make. Just then the passenger train came along, slowly, and the moose jumped off the tracks and ran along beside the train until he was on the other side of our creek, then he jumped back on the tracks right in front of the train and ran a short way before going off to the right and up onto a bench. The train crawled along at about two miles an hour and avoided hitting the moose. It was fun to watch. So far, we hadn't seen a bear, but the dogs had caught definite scents several times. We had six cans of moose meat left.

We had ordered a garden tiller from Sears earlier, and it finally came and Clyde was able to break the ground for our garden. But the tiller broke a part in the gear somewhere and had to be wired together. It wasn't made for breaking ground, after all, even though we had dug lots of it up with a shovel first. We had everything planted, and the lettuce, peas and radishes were up within ten days. We divided the existing rhubarb plants, and dug up some strawberry plants from across the tracks where the old section house used to be, and transplanted them next to the rhubarb.

Clyde's mom arrived on June 11th, and we were certainly happy that she came. She liked it about as much as we did, there in our beautiful valley, and had quite a time puttering in the garden and gathering wild greens and taking pictures.

Clyde put off going in to work until Mom came, but he went to town several days before she was due to arrive and put his job applications in all over town, anything that was available, and had several interviews. All of them could call him at Gold Creek when there was an opening, and he would go in on the next train. Then he met mom's flight, and brought her home on the train.

Two bears had been at Betty and Fred's tent - a cub climbed up and tore a long narrow place near the top, and a big bear ripped an eighteen inch square piece above the couch and left a few claw marks on the couch too. We pinned up the hole, tied tin cans with gravel in them all around the tent and set some small traps out hoping to discourage any more ripping. Clyde saw the bears, but they were too far away to shoot one. We knew if we didn't get them pretty soon, there wouldn't be much left of the tent, or of anything inside.

It rained incessantly for about a week, and we got a lot of school done. Soon there were only seven more days left - I felt greatly encouraged by that. We got a nice Northwinds message from my parents on our birthdays and anniversary. It was our eleventh anniversary and we had a quiet celebration.

Chapter 12 Summer On The Homestead

O n the first day of summer, June 21st, we had 24 hours of daylight, the longest day of the year. From then on the days would get shorter by a few minutes each day.

Clyde shot his first bear, and before the bear, he got a porcupine. We were glad to get the fresh meat. How do you skin a porcupine? VERY CAREFULLY! It was good, tasting a little like rabbit, a little like turkey. Bear meat was good too. Clyde's bear was a young one, tender and not very fat, about two years old. It tasted like lean fresh pork with a sort of sweet flavor and is very rich meat. I cooked the ribs and back meat for the dogs, and canned some of the rest of the meat in pint jars.

Lovel kids boating at the little pond

Louis and Mabel were here the day Clyde shot his bear and of course Mom had to run right out and snap a picture of it, even though it was a small one, as bears go. Mom and Mabel took to each other right away. Mabel was such a sweetheart.

It had been rainy and cloudy almost ever since Mom arrived. We only had four more days of school left and then FREEDOM for the rest of the summer!

One night the puppies were making a racket and I looked out, but didn't see anything and since Johnnie wasn't barking I thought nothing was there. The next day I discovered porcupine quills in Johnnie's right front foot and lower lip. So then I knew what the racket had all been about. I managed to pull the quills out of Johnnie's foot, but could only get three out of his lower lip. That was all he would let me pull, and since Clyde had gone to town to work, I needed to send a message to him or get help from someone else. So I wrote him a letter and he came home along with Betty and Fred, to help them put a roof on their cabin and salvage whatever they could from their tent.

It took all four of us to hold Johnnie down, while Clyde pulled out all the quills; we had to hog tie the poor dog. What a strong dog he was! He suffered no infection, and recovered completely. Unfortunately he did not learn a lesson from that encounter, and never kept away from porcupines. We had many a quill-pulling session over the years.

Louis shot a bear right beside Fred's tent; probably the same one that had ripped the tent apart. We canned 17 cans of that bear, steaks, and stew meat, ate some fresh and cooked the rest to feed to the dogs. I skinned the bear myself and did a good job, if I do say so. Mom Lovel has had quite a good sampling of nothing but wild meat since she arrived.

While Clyde was home, he caught a 17-inch rainbow trout at the mouth of our creek, and I took the train on a Saturday with Mabel, up to Indian River where I caught a 12-inch rainbow trout, but Mabel didn't catch any. And so we had trout for lunch that day. Fresh and yummy. Mabel told me that the salmon would be in soon, and fishing would be better.

Clyde went back to work, for the Alaska Railroad, on an extra gang. He and Fred finished the roof on Fred's cabin and moved the things out of their ruined tent. The garden was coming along slowly; it had been cool and cloudy so far all spring.

Debbie, Clyde, Shelley, Lisa and Bud Lovel the proud fishermen

My parents sent a Northwind message to Lisa on her third birthday, June 22nd. She was tickled pink to get her very own personal message on the radio.

By mid July we were able to harvest some vegetables from our garden, even though we had a miserable cold rainy summer. We had been able to eat lettuce; radishes, green onions and rhubarb, and the strawberries were blooming like crazy in spite of the rain, and getting some berries on the plants. We thought that soon we could pick some ripe berries.

Clyde sent a letter on the northbound passenger train telling us he was working on the extra gang at Willow, and needed a sleeping bag and a pillow. He said they would be moving around here and there all summer. I packed up a box with extra sweaters and socks along with the sleeping bag and pillow and the kids and I took it to the tracks when it was time for the southbound passenger train to come. I flagged the train down and six or eight tourists took our pictures.

Before the weeds and brush got so thick around the bridge, tourists would take our pictures at our 'home laundry' by the creek. We had an old stove down there, and the smoke from the stove kept the mosquitoes away as well as heating the wash water. I did all the washing in the old round washtub, which we also used as a bathtub, and an old-fashioned scrub board. The water from the creek was so cold it wouldn't get the clothes clean, no matter how hard I scrubbed; and besides, it made all the bones in my arms and hands ache. Heating the water a little helped a lot. With all the rain we'd had, the laundry never got dry anyway.

Home Laundry by the creek

All the kids passed their grades with good marks and were promoted to the fifth, fourth and second grades respectively. We would get their books to start school again by September. I was not in any hurry and neither were the kids, I knew.

Mom Lovel was very sick for several days, and once she stopped taking a few medications she began feeling better. It must have been the combination of pills upsetting her. She stayed in bed for several days and I didn't know what we would do if she got really sick, or how we would get her to a doctor or anything. It was kind of scary because there was nothing here at all, in the way of medical help or in case of an emergency. But after two days she was up and around and feeling better than she had felt for months, she said. She planned to go back to her home in Missouri in three or four weeks.

It continued to rain, rain, rain. The kids went out and played in the rain and it didn't seem to faze them at all. But I had to keep a fire in one of the stoves all the time to keep the damp and chill out of the house. Thank heavens Clyde got the roof fixed. At least we didn't have any leaks to contend with.

We received another 'care' package from my folks, and this one contained new underwear for all the kids, and socks and lots of sweet goodies as well as assorted packaged mixes and dry cereals. All treats.

At Gold Creek with Nellie & Mabel   **Waiting for the train**

In spite of the almost constant rain, the garden continued to grow. Mom said she had never seen anything like it. The peas were all making pods, and the potatoes were all in bloom.

How we all missed Clyde! He hadn't been home for two weekends by that time, and he wrote that he wouldn't be able to come home for two more weekends. They were working six days a week, ten hours a day, which meant lot of overtime pay. We were going to try to buy a tractor of some kind, and wanted to pay cash for it, so the overtime would mean we could get it that much quicker.

He was in a place called Hunter, as remote as Sherman; no roads, just the railroad. He wrote that the trip down there was beautiful, even though it was raining. It was somewhere south of Anchorage. He said the train winds around like a goat trail, through mountain passes, and near where they were camped was a high cascading waterfall, ending in a pool, complete with beaver houses and beaver. He said they would be there two and a half weeks, having seven miles of track to build up and move, from where it was sunk by The Earthquake. In its present sunken location, repairs had been tremendous, so the track would have to be moved.

We had been getting lots of green onions, radishes, lettuce and spinach from the garden and some of the turnips were big enough to eat, but the green beans had sort of shriveled up. It had been too cold and rainy for them and they just shivered and shrunk and died. The beets and carrots were finally growing and would be ready to eat soon. The cabbages were all small, but we planted them rather late, I feared.

Bud & Debbie in potato field   **Bud in the Cabbage patch**

Our "creek" became a roaring raging river; also the Susitna River was really bank full. The salmon pool was part of the river by then, and I doubted we would be able to get salmon from it, like we had last fall. It was too full and running too swiftly. But we planned to go up to Indian River instead and get our salmon there, with Mabel.

With all the rain there had been many mud slides on the tracks south of here, keeping Louis and Bill and the crew from Curry busy seven days a week. We seemed to be having what the natives called "little winter" that summer, instead of summer.

At the end of August, Clyde came home, finally. We all had missed him so much, but they had to work so much overtime to get finished down there before freeze-up that he hadn't been able to come home. They would be moving north in a few weeks, perhaps near here, Clyde said, maybe even on Sherman siding, which would have certainly been nice, but did not happen. He had written that he was bringing a large black bear hide home. He shot the bear near where they were camped, and had been drying the hide to bring home.

The kids, Mom and I all went to the river when the water went down a bit to see if the salmon were in the side pools yet; the water had cleared up in the pools and they were teeming with fish. Mostly 'dog' salmon, really chums, but they were called dog salmon because they had teeth, and fangs like a dog. They are larger than pink salmon. The kids waded into the pools and caught three of them by the tails and dragged them out; Mom snagged one with a fish hook, and a fellow from Fairbanks named Scotty, camped near here on leave, came by and joined us. He shot three of them with a .22 pistol.

We had a real fish fry, which made Mom very happy, and Scotty and his buddy Bill, also from Fairbanks, came for dinner. We ate four of the salmon, and gave Mabel the other three and left the rest for later, in the pools. I thought I might can some if I had time. But by then the strawberries were ripe, and the wild currants, and cranberries, and there was jelly to be made, potatoes to dig, and everything else to be done, all at once. I didn't know if I would get any fish canned or not.

Scotty and Bill were both in the Army, stationed at Fairbanks, on leave and bear hunting. They were camped out near Betty and Fred's place. The reason they got off the train there was because the conductor told them that a lot of bear seemed to be in that area. I expected they would be over often, as they didn't like their own cooking, much, and they both seemed to enjoy playing with the kids, who all certainly liked them. They were both really nice boys, and helpful as far as chopping wood and heavy water hauling. They pitched right in, gladly.

Mom had decided it was time for her to go home. I think the constant rain had finally gotten her down. But she planned to leave on the 12th of September, and when Clyde came home, she told him, and we figured out what kind of a schedule we would have to keep to get her into town. Scotty and Bill offered to move their camp here and feed the dogs so we could all go in on the train.

Mabel and Louis came down and Mabel begged us to let Lisa come and stay with her - she so wanted a little girl! And Lisa loved to play with their boys too, so our plans were all made. Mabel came down to get Lisa on the 10th, and that afternoon, after Scotty and Bill came, we caught the train to town. We told them to move in to the house, since it was still raining, and they did.

On the way in to town, a sleazy old drunk guy came staggering down the aisle of the train, and stopped by our seat, and started stroking Mom's hair, which mortified her nearly to death, and told her what beautiful hair he thought she had. The conductor made him move on, much to our relief.

It was Bud's birthday again, and we had actually spent one whole year out on the homestead, already. We really had something to celebrate. Clyde met us at our motel in Anchorage, the next day, and took us out for dinner, and even though it was a bit late, we had our celebration. It was Bud's ninth birthday, already, and Clyde and I realized that our kids were growing up, faster than we ever thought they would. Poor Bud, two years in a row with a late birthday party! He really didn't mind.

We spent the rest of the day visiting and driving around looking at sights, and enjoying ourselves. The kids and I had to take the train for home Sunday morning, the 12th. It was the last daily train for the summer, and we knew that Scotty and Bill would be taking this train for Fairbanks, too, since their three weeks leave was over.

Clyde and Mom spent the day together and Clyde saw Mom off at the airport Sunday evening before going back to Seward to work. The railroad had sent the extra gang further south instead of north, and so he was farther away than ever at that time.

The same bunch was on the train going back as had been on when we went in to town, most of them suffering from severe hangovers, too. The man who had so admired Mom's hair was extremely sorry if he had offended either one of us, and he apologized to me for both of us, over and over again. He seemed to be a very nice man, when sober.

The further we got from Anchorage, the sunnier it was, and when we got home, it was beautiful. No clouds, or rain. Scotty and Bill got on the train as we got off, and we all said good-bye and thanked them for taking care of the dogs and everything. They said everything had been fine, and that they would write. Also they asked if they could come back on their next leave, and they said they would not tell anyone how nice it was here, either, so we wouldn't be over-run with hunters. They didn't get a bear, but enjoyed themselves anyway.

The house was beautifully cleaned, dishes all done, dogs all fine, and they had left a box of food and a note saying again, how much they enjoyed our hospitality, and that if they came again, they would bring all kinds of goodies with them.

Shortly after we got home, Mabel and Louis came with Lisa. Mabel said she had been very good, except for the first night, and Lisa wanted to go back to Gold Creek, with them. Lisa caught a cold from Mabel's kids who caught theirs from her cousin's kids from town. So we all got Lisa's cold and felt pretty miserable all week. But we survived, and I thought we should have brought Lisa with us to town, anyway.

The sun shone here all the time we were in town, and stayed sunny until Tuesday, two days after we got home, and then started raining again. But the kids and I dug all the potatoes while the sun was still shining. There were quite a few good sized ones in the patch nearest the creek.

Lisa with the potato harvest 1974

When the freight came the following week, the lumber and tar paper for the roof on the room Clyde was building came and when he got home the next Saturday he put the roof on, even though it was raining. He said at least it was on, even though it was damp. The new chimney we had ordered for the barrel stove was not on that freight. We hoped it would come on the next one.

It really seemed lonesome around here with Mom gone, and Clyde too. But I had much too much to do to dwell on it for long. I painted the kitchen and also around all the windows in the house, inside and out. It looked better, at least. Then stuffed all the cracks with oakum. As long as it was raining, I worked inside the house, trying to help make it less drafty for the coming winter.

We got a very nice letter from Bill, for both he and Scotty, thanking us for our "wonderful hospitality and good eats", a nice long letter, mostly to the kids. They were thrilled, of course. He said they would be back down when they get their next time off. He also said that all the way back to Fairbanks on the train, the sun was shining - it made them both sick.

We heard again from Clyde; his gang had been moved almost all the way down to Seward, and he had no idea when he would get home again unless they cut them to five days pretty soon. They were scheduled to move up above Anchorage in three or four weeks, and would be working this section all winter, and also next summer. But Clyde, along with two thirds of the gang, were all hired on as temporary hires, so he had no idea how long he would be working.

Mary fishing at the mouth of Sherman creek

It really was quiet around here with no trains. Most of the freights came at night by then, and only one through freight each day, either northbound or southbound. Only the "local freight" still came at about the same time - anywhere from 4:30 PM to 9:00 PM. Then there was the weekend passenger train, one going north on Saturdays and one going south on Sundays. The one train in the middle of the week was a night train, so we didn't even see those, since they passed by here in the wee hours of the morning.

Mabel crocheted beautiful things, and she had convinced Mom that she would love to make her a suit, if Mom would buy the yarn, so before Mom left Alaska, Mabel took her measurements and Mom bought the yarn before she left Anchorage, and gave it to me to give to

Mabel. She got a beautiful, rich shade of brown and a creamy tan contrast color.

Mom (Ethel) Lovel's birthday party

Bud in the turnips

Mabel got the yarn when she brought Lisa back, and was working on the suit; she loved doing that sort of thing; I wouldn't have the patience. It only took Mabel three weeks, and she came down from Gold Creek to visit, with Mom's suit all finished! What a fast worker she was, and it certainly was a work of art. It was simply beautiful. I knew Mom would be thrilled with it. Mabel wanted to show it to me before she mailed it off to Mom. She told me how much she loved Mom and how her boys all called her their "Gramma". She said she appreciated Mom so much because she treated Mabel like a human being, not condescendingly like so many white people do just because she's an Eskimo. She felt as though Mom was a true friend to her, bless her heart. She was such a neat lady! She was going to write to Mom also, which I knew would please Mom greatly.

Chapter 13 Winter, Already?

I t snowed on the mountains all around on the 25th of September, and there was a real nip in the air. After such a miserable summer of cold and rain, I wondered if the rest of the summers would be as bad. If so, how would we ever get our required acreage cleared and planted in time? I thought they really needed to revise the homestead laws to fit this state.

We got busy picking cranberries and rose hips and canning the juice for later use as jelly and syrup or punch. Clyde came home for a few days to finish putting the tarpaper on the roof of the new room. He had thirty-six hours of sick leave coming so he planned to use some of it to get his teeth fixed, as well while he was off.

Fred came up to fix his roof and the whole cabin, sleeping bags and everything was soaked, so he came and spent Saturday night here. He said they still plan to move up the first of November.

Ice formed on the rain tubs every morning and it never got warmer than 40 degrees during the days so it was a bit chilly picking berries. But we kept warm with our good old barrel stove.

Clyde had a hard time getting back to the crew - he got a ride with a man from a road camp to Moose pass and got soaked through before he reached the extra gang cars. The work had slowed down a lot and they were talking about laying off for the winter. He actually only worked until mid-October and then came the layoff. But he was home again, at last, and we were all happy. The railroad people told him he would be able to get on again in the spring, but he hoped to get another job in the meantime. He had put his application in everywhere before leaving town to come home, and arranged with several friends to send him a 'Northwinds' message if any openings happened where they worked. He planned, meanwhile, to run a trap line with Buddy. Louis said he would show them how. Meanwhile, it looked like we would have a long, lean winter.

It snowed about eight inches, and then we had clear skies, sunny days and freezing weather. It got down to zero or below at night and up to 20 above during the day. Having had only about seven or eight days of sun all summer, we were all a bit run down, as we all got colds, except Shelley and Lisa. Debbie was the first; she caught her cold from Betty when they moved up from town and Clyde caught his from Debbie and I from him and then Bud got his last. But we slowly recovered and really were enjoying the sun shining through the windows and helping to keep the house warm.

I made all new harnesses for all the dogs, except Tanny. He met his untimely end when he tried to drag Lisa under the house and nearly succeeded braining her. Clyde quickly and mercifully put him away.

We came to the conclusion that we would have to use the money we had been saving for the tractor to live on until Clyde got work, but I was so glad to have him home. School took up so much of the day that the chores suffered. At least we still had carrots, onions and potatoes, canned salmon and all sorts of dried food we had been stocking up on ever since Clyde first went to work.

We saw a lovely big bull moose across the river, but before I could get the camera out he was gone. We hoped to get a moose soon. Second season was opening in about 10 days.

Clyde finished the room addition on the north side of the house, finally, and we were using it for storing firewood to begin with. He put plastic over the window instead of glass and the door was hung, and the walls were draped with plastic and cardboard, and the boards from the walls of the dog pen were on the floor. It really was a help to have that room. The house was much warmer; no wind got in at all on the north end. It made great insulation for that side of the house.

By that time, the old wood cookstove had so many holes it was unsafe to use, and burned the wood and coal up too fast, so Clyde made me a barrel stove to cook on. That way he wouldn't have to cut the wood in short pieces. He had the top all flattened out and I had a portable oven to sit on top and we tried it. The metal-bestos chimney we ordered never came; we canceled the order, since there was an old rusty heavy metal water pipe in a ditch at Curry, which Louis got for us. We put it up outside after Clyde cut a hole and ran the existing stovepipe into it. The barrel cookstove worked fairly well, but it was slow cooking on it, and I really preferred the old cookstove. Too bad it was so full of holes. The barrel stove got so hot it ran us out of the kitchen; we had to get it really hot in order to cook on it. But it saved on propane gas, anyway.

Soon we had 18 inches of snow, and had been running the dogs and getting them in shape for trapping. They were hauling in loads of wood from the piles out in the woods, and the room addition was nearly full.

We all piled in the dogsled and with Clyde on back riding the runners, we went the three quarters of a mile to Betty and Fred's. The dogs actually pulled all of us! It was fun. Fred was putting up the other half of their cabin.

We were busy with school again, and my weekends were totally taken up with things like baking, laundry, and trying to get mittens and socks knitted. With the new harnesses and the new sled the dogs were working out well. Clyde and the kids all ran them, every day after school, and hauled in wood or ran down to Betty and Fred's.

Bud, Clyde & Lisa Mushing Winter 1964-65

Everyone in both our families sent packages, with warm clothes and food and odds and ends of fun things for the kids, which I hid away to wrap up for Christmas. My mom sent some cake and cookie mixes, and Shelley could hardly wait to try them out. I had been teaching her to cook, and she really wanted to learn. The cake mixes, I thought, should be easy, if I could just convince her to read and follow the directions first.   Sometimes Shelley surprises us with breakfast in bed, which reminded me of my younger days - I guessed I was getting old. I was nearly 30!

My Grandma sent some clothes she made for all four kids - warm flannel pajamas, shirts, nice things which I also put away to wrap for Christmas, so the kids' Christmas wouldn't be so lean. We didn't have much money left, and Clyde wasn't going in to look for work until January, after the first. He had been looking for a moose, but so far, no luck. We really needed the meat bad.

It had turned cold - five degrees above zero to 15 degrees below zero all the time. There was only about two feet of snow on the ground. We had clear skies every day, though it was only daylight for about five and a half hours with no sun, only the light from it.

The dogs had shaped up to a really good team so far. The three pups and Johnnie worked very well together and really got the woodpiles in fast. The room was about half full, floor to ceiling, and we really burned a lot to keep warm, in that weather.

We were down to one sack of dog food, and two sacks of cornmeal. I cooked a mush of cornmeal, adding all the leftover cooking grease and dog food. If we didn't get a moose soon, I didn't know what we would feed the dogs, and we really needed them. The two females pulled like crazy, and seemed to be untiring, but they didn't know the usual directional commands of 'gee, haw, and whoa' like Johnnie and Copper. Whenever any of the pups goofed off, Johnnie would growl and snap at them and that's all it seemed to take - they all knew who was boss.

Mrs. Lobdell, the minister's wife in Talkeetna, sent up two big boxes of clothes for the kids, which the minister dropped off the train one Saturday. There was a note in the box, which said that she couldn't use any of the clothes, that people kept giving her things all the time, and none of them would fit her children, so she thought we could use them. They all fit our kids, and out of the lot Debbie got seven pairs of nearly new jeans, Shelley got four pairs, Lisa two, and Bud five. There were sweaters galore for all of them and pajamas and all kinds of nice warm stuff. So the kids were definitely all set with enough clothes to last the winter, at least.

We met Reverend and Mrs. Lobdell for the first time on the train when we were going into Anchorage with Mom Lovel in September, and became friends. They were nice, and had cute kids too, and well mannered. We weren't members of their church, but they dropped off a note now and then and a Sunday school paper for our kids. I think Reverend Lobdell rode the train to different small communities here and there to hold church services once a month or every two weeks; I couldn't remember which it was, but he did tell us.

The creek was rapidly freezing dry by that time, and I was so busy with tests all that week I didn't have time to answer letters or anything. Debbie would go out on the dog sled with Clyde while I was administering tests; her tests came at a different time.

Fred and a friend of his, Frank, finished the cabin, so it was a whole cabin by then, but not very warm, Betty said, because the logs were too small, and green, and it was cold on the floor, and too warm up above. They were going to get another stove.

Mom Lovel wrote to say that she was crazy about the suit Mabel made for her; it fit perfectly and Mom loved it. Mabel thought it would have been prettier made in the tan yarn and trimmed in the brown, but I thought it was gorgeous, and so did Mom.

We asked Betty and Fred to come for Thanksgiving dinner, but they said they wanted to spend their first Thanksgiving and Christmas alone in their little cabin, so they did, and we did too. It seemed a bit strange, since we were used to family and friends gathering at Thanksgiving and Christmas time.

We had a nice Thanksgiving anyway, even though we didn't have a traditional one of ham, turkey or moose. I had managed to save a little bacon, and made Spanish rice with all of the bacon in it, and fresh bread. It tasted very good, and we had a lot to be thankful for. We all piled on the dog sled and went to Betty and Fred's and brought them a loaf of fresh bread. They had hamburger for dinner.

Buddy was doing very well in school, though it was really hard for him and took him twice as long as the other kids to finish an assignment, mostly because he was so restless, and being a boy, I was sure he would rather be running the dogs, or chopping wood or hunting with his dad or anything else besides school.

Bud did great with the dogs. He ran Johnnie and Copper together, sometimes, and Chena too, though I thought then that three were a bit too much for him alone. When we hooked up more than two of them, either Debbie or Shelley went along to help in case they got tangled or anything. Both females really did pull, harder than the males, who after the first two or three trips liked to goof off a little and slow down. But when they were hooked up with the females, they didn't get a chance to slow down.

The weather warmed up to 20 or 30 degrees and we had a couple of good chinooks, (which are warm winds), and some of the snow melted. But then it turned colder, and we were treated to a spectacular display of northern lights, all colors and shapes. It was gorgeous. After that it snowed heavily for a few days, making what there was of daylight very dim indeed. We had to burn lamps all day.

Clyde shot a fat porcupine, and I managed to make two good meals out of it.

We had only $56. left, and then Louis brought our mail, and everyone had sent money! Both our families wanted us to succeed in this venture and dream of ours; my folks sent a check, my sister sent one, Clyde's Mom sent one and my Grandma too. It was wonderful. None of the checks were large, but all together they amounted to a lot. We compiled a Christmas grocery order and sent it off, thanks to both our generous families.

Even though it was snowing, the kids would run out to play in it as soon as school was finished each day. We had about three feet by then, and Buddy would stand up on a log, fall backwards into drifts of snow so deep that he got buried, and plow his way out and do it again. The girls went diving in and out of the drifts too, following the puppies.

The night our Christmas grocery order came, it was very late, and very cold with winds blowing about 30 to 40 miles per hour. The snow was drifted deep over the path to the railroad tracks; we had a terrible time getting the groceries up to the house in the sled. Even the dogs could make no headway in the deep drifts. The strong gusts of wind would practically knock us over, and we floundered to our waists in the deep drifts. So we ended up wrestling the sled ourselves on snowshoes. It took us over an hour to make two trips and we were both exhausted. The kids were all in bed sound asleep during this time.

The next day we got another package from my folks with oranges, apples, and packages wrapped up for Christmas, and the fresh fruit was all in splendid condition. My mother really knew how to pack! Everything was perfect with our grocery order too - not one thing left out. In fact, the Teelands even included a box of chocolate covered cherries and one of their calendars, a nice Christmas present. Those Teelands were really wonderful people.

When the weather calmed down a bit, we all went out into the woods and picked out a Christmas tree and brought it home to decorate. At that time it looked like we wouldn't have any company to share our Christmas with.

A friend in town sent up a box of toys for the kids and we had no idea what was in the box because it said not to open until Christmas. But it was a big box; and a few days before Christmas Charlie, Clyde's old boss from the railroad gang stopped and left a box with a card from him and Olive saying, "Just a touch of Christmas Cheer for the Lovel Family." They had been parked on the siding and were moving out. In the box was a beautiful date and raisin-nut cake frosted with white icing and trimmed with pecan halves; a three pound coffee can filled with home-made fudge and crispy candy, and a dozen and a half oranges. Were we ever surprised, to say the least. I had never even met them, and we hadn't been down to the switch to see them since the weather was so bad. The freight that brought our groceries picked up the gang cars and so I wrote a thank you note to them and mailed it when possible. I would rather have been able to thank them in person, though. And the following year we did finally get to do that.

Christmas morning the track patrolman at that time, Johnny Blidburg came by on the gas car, loaded to the brim with bags of goodies. He gave us a bag with an apple, an orange, a banana, some candy and nuts for each member of the family. He was bringing everybody all along the line the same thing, he said, and didn't make it back until 11 PM, so he didn't have dinner with us, but he did stop for coffee and pie. He was happy as could be; said he'd had a wonderful time playing Santa and it was the best Christmas he'd ever had.

Shelley and I walked down to Betty and Fred's cabin and brought them a little cake I made with pink frosting and little candy canes on top and asked them once again if they wouldn't change their minds and come have dinner with us. But they said "no", however they did say they would come for New Years. Betty had color books and crayons for the kids. She said Olive and Charlie gave them a box of goodies just like ours. We followed the 1:30 passenger train home and a couple of the guys from the extra gang who were friends of Clyde's waved at us. When we got home, the train had stopped and left off a box from them and there were ten pounds of hard candy and about the same of nuts, a canned ham, oranges, apples, bananas and pears. Also ski skates for Debbie and Shelley, two planes for Bud and a pounding peg set for Lisa. We were certainly surprised! With all the other presents from all the family and friends, the kids didn't even know we were poor!

For Christmas dinner we had a glazed ham with pineapple, corn-on-the-cob, mashed potatoes and ham gravy, candied sweet potatoes, Jello salad, green beans, pumpkin and apple pies, hot rolls, and the usual goodies. We wished that all our family, my folks and Clyde's could have been with us, but we did get Northwinds messages from them, which somehow made them seem closer.

The day after Christmas, to top off all the wonderful things that happened that day, Clyde shot a nice young bull moose. He was out on snowshoes scouting for tracks to begin setting traps, and saw the trail of blood. He followed it to the river and across. In the bushes on the other side was the moose, wounded from the early morning freight train, evidently. It had dragged itself across the frozen river and was stuck in a drift in the brush. Clyde shot it, gutted it out and hung it up by quarters in the trees and came home to tell us of the luck. He was a bit leery of crossing the river, but where a moose could go, a human could too. The next morning we went over with the dogs and hauled back all the meat, and the head too, to use for bait for trapping. We left at daylight, Bud, Clyde and I, and all the dogs. It took us two trips. The dogs got the mangled front leg, where the train hit it, and we brought the other front quarter to Betty and Fred and kept the hindquarters for ourselves, which gave us enough meat to last for several months, at least.

Mabel and Louis finally got the generator they had been waiting for, for over a year, from the railroad, to replace the one that burned up.

They got it put in when it came in October, and a shack built for it, and got it up and running around the end of October. It was a used generator, but seemed like a good one. The first week of January it burned up also, along with the generator shack, twenty gallons of diesel fuel, the meat shed, tool shed and both outhouses. Mabel was alone when it caught fire, and she called everyone with a phone she could think of. Johnny Blidburg picked Clyde up on his way to Gold Creek, and the man up north of Gold Creek met Louis working on the track and told him what was happening, and they all got there together. By that time everything was burned to the ground. But no one was hurt, and the section house was not hurt at all, and it was a good thing Louis had his gasoline and kerosene stored in the big sheds out front by the tracks or all of Gold Creek would have been burned to the ground. Poor Mabel was so mad - both generators they were sent they only got to use for two months and then they burned up. Mabel told Clyde that she guessed it was time she left Gold Creek. Their oldest boy would be of school age by September, and Mabel didn't want to teach him herself. I really missed having her for a neighbor when they moved to town.

Clyde went to Anchorage mid-January, just after the sun peeked over the tip of the mountain for the first time in over two months, and got a job the very next day, on the Air Force Base, doing Civil Service work. He sent us a Northwinds message, which gave us hope that we could get the new tractor we needed so desperately. We had to have something to plow and clear the land with. At least by that time, we had plenty of firewood cut and Clyde would again be coming home weekends, to do whatever he could so that we would be okay while he was gone. In a letter he sent later he told us when he got paid he would be home. His job was only a six-month temporary position with a possibility of extension for six more months. If any permanent jobs opened up, he would transfer to one of those. Once more we would have an income. It was awfully hard living without money. Meanwhile, Clyde had his application in with the Railroad, and he hoped to one day be able to work close to home.

Those kids of ours, I couldn't make them wear shoes or boots. When a train came, they dashed out the door, barefoot, or in stocking feet, right in to the snow to wave at the trains. Why they never got frostbite, I never understood, but they stayed healthy anyway. They all had shoes, slippers, and snow boots, and when I tried to make them stop to slip something on their feet, they would just say, "But Mom, we will miss the trains if we stop to put on our shoes!" and ran out the door barefoot. I supposed they jumped up and down enough to keep from freezing their feet.

Louis and Bill looked out for us again while Clyde was gone. They stopped by every day, nearly, and came up to the house for coffee. They both said if I needed anything at all, just give a call. If anything came up I needed help with, I could go to the train phone down the tracks by the siding, in a little booth and call the dispatcher in Anchorage. He would then call Louis on the telephone and let him know we needed help.

Clyde stayed with a man he used to work with, who lived alone in a small trailer in Anchorage. Clyde paid half the rent and utilities, and had his name on the list for sleeping quarters on the base, which would have been cheaper, but it never came to pass.

It was a full time job and a half, keeping the fires going all day and night and teaching three grades of school, hauling up sled loads of ice every other day from the creek with the kids help, of course, and the dogs pulling the sled. The ice was for drinking water, and we melted snow, again, for all other water needs. Most of the days were cloudy, and though we had not seen the sun because of the clouds, we knew it was there, somewhere.

So many things happened and always when Clyde was gone! Debbie fell and stuck a very rusty nail about half an inch into her leg. That was on a Tuesday morning, and I flagged down Johnny on his way back to Curry running his patrol. He called Louis when he reached Curry. Louis called the dispatcher in Anchorage, who then called Clyde. Then Tuesday night we got a Northwinds message from Clyde to put Debbie on Thursday's four am train. Later Tuesday night, Johnny came by with some medicine and advice from the new Roadmaster's wife. They lived in Curry, 10 miles South of us, and she was an R.N. I had thought Clyde could get a doctor to send up a tetanus shot, and Mrs. Valentine offered to come up with Johnny Wednesday morning and give the shot to Debbie. But no doctor would send a shot up.

We got a note on Tuesday night's train from Clyde that the tickets for Debbie were all arranged, and the conductor would look after her. Debbie was so excited to be going to town all by herself, and the other kids were green with envy, of course. We got her off okay, and got a Northwinds message again on Thursday night that she arrived safely and all was fine. It turned out that Mrs. Valentine went to town on the same train, so she sat with Debbie the whole time. Of course Debbie came back on Saturday with Clyde, all big and important and full of the news of her big adventure in town, and her new friend, Mrs. Valentine. Another friend kept Debbie during the day while Clyde was at work Thursday and Friday. Debbie saw a doctor and got her shot. Meanwhile, Mrs. Valentine's doctor gave her a good supply of tetanus booster, penicillin, and other medications, which might be necessary, also needles, sutures and whatever else might be needed in case of emergencies. She had two small children, as well. Debbie's leg was fine, and healed nicely with no infection

Clyde got a lot of work done that Saturday, but it snowed all day Sunday and Sunday night, a full 24 inches. But Saturday night, it was too warm in the house, and we opened the kitchen door for a while. The kids were all asleep. Clyde and I were sitting on the couch in the kitchen and an ermine walked in; he just walked right in like he owned the place, and began scurrying around examining everything, and Clyde and I sat very still and talked to it. Unafraid, it scampered up and sniffed our shoes, sat down, looked us over, then did a few flips and sauntered out the door again. That was some show. It was probably the same ermine that had been out in back by Chena during the summer, and it would sit up on a log and screech at Chena until she barked and ran at it, and then it would do a back flip off the log and chatter and tease until Chena got tired of the whole thing, always just out of reach. Feisty little devil, but so cute, with it's bright shiny beady little black eyes.

That weekend Clyde and I talked a lot about whether he should come home every weekend or save the money towards the tractor. We decided that he needed to come home every weekend; otherwise we would be sacrificing all family life together. If he didn't come home every weekend, he would just have to spend every minute he was at home cutting wood or there wouldn't be any for summer use, or for the next winter. We talked about a lot of things, and to us, our family life was the most important, and not to be sacrificed.

More "care" packages came from my folks containing fresh lemons, soup mixes, vitamins, potato chips, cheeses and other goodies.

Clyde's mom sent us a Northwinds message on Valentines Day, and some Mendets, along with a valentine. Mendets were the neatest little things ever invented, to mend holes in pots, pans, washtubs, anything metal, plastic, rubber or whatever; they consisted of varied sizes of little short screw-like things, cork washers, and metal washers, along with tiny nuts, and a two ended tool, one end sharp and pointed to 'round out' the hole, and the other end fit the little nuts, to screw the whole thing in place. The idea was to find a screw as near the size of the hole in the object you were mending, force it into the hole with a cork washer next to the pan-body, and a metal washer on the other side of the hole. Then put on the nut and tighten it. I really went wild and used up nearly a whole package mending two washtubs, the metal washbasin and a dishpan. I hated leaky pans and things, and those Mendets were certainly nice to have around. Also, they worked, and where the hole had been, never leaked again.

The weather turned very cold, 20 degrees below zero most nights and clear, with northern lights nearly every night. It warmed up to 10 to 15 degrees above zero during the day when the sun was out, for an hour or so.

The kids and I discovered wolverine tracks after the dogs barked and barked the night before. We could even hear Pal barking from way down at Betty and Fred's cabin. The wolverine came fairly near the dogs, and really drove them wild. The tracks were very clear. We looked them up in our book of "Wild Animal Tracks".

When the freight came, my eagerly expected tank of propane was on it, and so I could bake yeast bread and rolls as much as the kids wanted, which amounted to at least three loaves a day. Bud and I went down to Betty and Fred's cabin on the dog sled the day before the freight was due, to ask Fred if he would come up after the freight to help me with the gas tank, and he did. We loaded it on the sled and the dogs pulled it up to the house. Fred hooked it up for me, then discovered a slight leak. Clyde fixed that leak when he came home the following weekend. One of the fittings was cracked and Clyde put a new one on. Meanwhile, before Clyde got it fixed, I just turned the tank off after each use.

At that time, the last moose quarter we had was hanging in the house thawing, dripping in the big tub. When it was thawed enough, I cut steaks and roasts out of it and with the meat we already had wrapped and stored in the old washing machine outside, we had enough for about six weeks. I had been using the old washing machine, with no motor, as a freezer. It was mouse-proof, and other animal proof, with the lid weighted down with heavy logs so the wind could not blow it off, or an animal knock it off. It worked very well.

We were still hauling ice from the creek, and wood from the new woodpile across the tracks just at the bend near the house. I got enough exercise that I could eat all the yeast bread and rolls I wanted to and not gain weight. It was great. We had not had any colds or flu, even though we heard on the radio there was a flu epidemic in Anchorage.

Clyde took the laundry to town with him each week, and did it for me at the laundromat, thereby freeing me up for schoolwork and cooking and all the rest. That was a very big help, not to mention that the clothes looked clean once again.

March 3rd was Shelley's 11th birthday, and I baked a cake and made snow ice cream, which was good, but not creamy and rich like 'store bought' as the kids called it. When Clyde came home that Saturday, he brought the "good stuff:" and we had another party.

Betty and Fred moved back to town early, for the summer. Betty really didn't like living out here, so far from everything. But they planned to use the cabin for weekends and vacations. They told us we were always welcome to stay at their place in town if we needed to, when we came in to shop or for errands.

When Louis and Bill stopped by for coffee and to see if we needed anything, Louis brought notes from Mabel, which I hastened to answer and send back with them. It had been too cold all winter to ride up and visit Mabel, or for her to come here, either. So she and I had visited by hand-delivered 'mail' all winter, except for just before Christmas when she and the boys came for a while.

Chena was due to have Johnnie's puppies around that time. Clyde advertised for homes for them, with no takers, and we certainly could not afford to feed any more dogs. We didn't know how many she would have, of course, but planned to keep only one, a male, if there was one, and find homes for the rest or put them to sleep. It was a sad decision to make, but necessary. So when she finally did have the pups, there were four of them, three females and only one male. We could not find anyone wanting a husky pup, so Clyde gently dispatched the females. I didn't have the courage to - they were all so cute and lovable. We knew we would eventually have to find a home for the grown females, probably both of them, if the male pup, which the kids decided to name "Yukon", turned out to be a good sled dog like his pa. By the time Yukon was two weeks old, he was as wide as he was long; being the only pup, he got all the milk. He sure was cute; several shades of gray, silver and black. He had the same markings around his eyes as Johnnie, and huge feet.

Near the end of March I received a letter from my mother telling of my dad's bout with flu, which turned into pneumonia and his subsequent hospitalization in an oxygen tent. Then she sent a Northwinds message that he was off the critical list, which was certainly a relief. With complications from the flu and heart damage from the pneumonia, Dad almost died. But Mom's Northwinds message said that he would be able to leave the hospital at the end of the week, if he kept improving. Poor Dad, I was so worried about him, and Mom- what a hard time she had coping with everything. I longed for a phone - it was so scary being so very far away from them and not knowing for sure just what was happening. We had a deposit paid for a phone, but were on a long waiting list to get one.

March 30th was Debbie's eighth birthday. She was growing up! They all were, too fast. We had a fun party, with cake and snow ice cream, presents we had hidden away, and part of her present was the trip to town, the following week, and a Walt Disney movie.

We were all packed and ready to go to town. We flagged the train down at 4 PM Sunday in front of our house. The Alaska Railroad is the only one left that will stop anywhere if a person waves an arm or piece of cloth, or at night, a light. At that time the maximum speed was 30 miles per hour. There was a potbellied coal stove in the caboose and engine for warmth, and was really rather quaint, but after nearly five hours of riding, just to go 141 miles, it did get a bit tiresome with the jerks and jolts, rattles and creaks. This was the train they called the "Streamliner". It was a little faster and a little warmer than dogsled travel though. Besides, the snow was getting too rotten to run the dogs on. They kept sinking in every few feet. We were having lovely spring weather - intermittent sunshine, snow storms, sunshine, sleet, sunshine, rain and hail, sunshine, more snow; but still the stumps were 'growing' every day as the level of the old snow kept dropping steadily. However, the creek was still hard as a brick, and we were still chopping our drinking water supply from it. Living like that certainly produced muscles.

When we were in town for that week early in April I called my parents and talked to both Mom and Dad. He was home from the hospital by then and feeling much better. It was great talking to them both and best of all that Dad was well once more.

We spent the time stocking up on supplies, also on garden seed and fertilizer. We planned to put in at least an acre of potatoes, and though the soil was rich, it seemed that nothing had time to decompose, and fertilizer was needed to supplement and warm the soil. The children had all been looking forward to the change of pace and a break from school. They had the chance to see their friends, go to a movie, spend their allowances and generally we all had a good time. The week went by rapidly, and we were all glad to be back home once again. It was a hectic week. The dogs were all fine, as Louis and Bill stopped by every day and fed them for us while we were gone.

Only seven more weeks of school left; none of us caught any germs in town, and we were looking forward to 'garden time'. We started some of the seeds in peat pots and flats, anxious for things to start growing.

Chapter 14 Disaster Strikes

Yukon was so big and fat and cute and funny. He looked like a fluffy gray, back and white St. Bernard pup. He was about five weeks old, when disaster struck. It was 2 am on a Tuesday morning in late April, and the dogs' frantic barking woke us up. I could hear Chena and Crissy fighting. They were both chained behind the house, near the woods. Johnnie and Copper were barking and I guess Chena and Crissy had been fighting for a long time. We had left Chena run loose because her chain had rubbed the hair off her neck and chest in places, and she had been loose for over a week. We didn't have to worry about her running off because of her pup, Yukon, in the doghouse. She was very possessive of the pup and stayed right by him all the time. But somehow, piecing it all together afterward, it seemed she somehow had managed to knock the logs off the washer lid we kept the moose meat in, and dragged a plastic bag full of meat past Crissy, left it by her (Chena's) doghouse and went back for more. This made Crissy so upset she broke her chain and, I guessed they started fighting then, because when I went out with the lantern, there was blood all over them both and all over the snow. Chena was in her house shielding the puppy, and Crissy was just outside, still fighting. Chena broke off one of her fangs inside Crissy's upper jaw, and it was sticking out the top of her nose and a piece of bone was sticking down through the roof of Crissy's mouth, besides half of an ear ripped off and a deep gouge in the side of her neck and two on her face. She kept pawing at her nose and shaking her head as I tied her up. Then I saw that Chena had her throat torn in a dozen places, and her jugular vein was punctured, because she was gurgling in her throat and choking on her own blood when I got out there. Also blood was shooting out of her neck in heavy spurts. There was absolutely nothing I could do to help either one of them, and rather than let them die slowly in agony, I shot them. I hope I never have to shoot another dog for any reason. It was awful. Why did these things seem to always happen when Clyde was gone?

Lisa & Debbie with Chena

At least Yukon was not hurt, and he was old enough to survive eating solid food. The kids promptly spoiled him. They fixed a box for him to sleep in on the porch, with the outside door open so he could get in and out, and he didn't even mess on the porch once. Which was a plus. He was a smart little rascal, fat as could be, and playful. He resembled Johnnie in every way except color. He had the same wolf - eyes too. He waddled out and played with Copper a lot - Johnnie just ignored him except to sniff him, but otherwise he was indifferent. We made a little sled out of a cardboard box and Yukon pulled it along behind him like a veteran. It was funny to watch.

Later that same week Louis stopped by just to tell me not to let the kids wander too far from the house, as there was a hungry grizzly bear just out of hibernation, wandering around looking for something to eat. Louis said it wasn't a very big one; the prints were the size of a large dinner plate. That sounded plenty big to me! We never saw it, or its tracks, but Louis said it was only two miles south of here, and headed this way. It must have gone across the river.

We had a lot of rain and wet snowfall for about a week, and warm weather, and then it turned colder at night after it cleared up, and the snow, what was left of it, became hard as concrete, so that we could walk everywhere on it. Then we got busy on the back woodpiles again, with the gun along, of course, and managed to get it all to the house in just a few days. We could only haul it in the mornings when the snow was still hard, but as each day wore on towards noon, the snow started giving way again, and we had to wait until the next morning to resume, after the cold at night froze the snow harder once again. Afternoons were spent finishing up schoolwork.

When Clyde came home the following weekend, he was happy we had been able to get all the wood in, especially since the snow was once more back to the rotten stage where we could go nowhere on it. He told me that he had been working all week, after work, helping a friend tear down the lean-to which had been built as an addition to his trailer, and move his trailer to a lot. Clyde got to keep all the useable lumber from the room, and he bundled it up and took it to the freight depot and it was shipped up on Wednesday, enough lumber to finish up the room, build a new outhouse and enclose the cellar, with maybe some studs left for the woodshed Clyde wanted to build.

The next Friday the kids and I went up to visit with Mabel at Gold Creek. It was a beautiful sunny day. We gabbed about everything under the sun, and walked up the tracks, which were snow-free, to Nellie's place. Nellie had been alone since February when her husband went to work at Adak. She gave me some seeds she didn't want; She had her flats planted too. She had been busy during the winter doing some beadwork and she showed us some of it, and it was really beautiful and intricate work. All those tiny beads! What patience it must have taken. It was a lovely day, and a much needed break for us all.

In all my spare time, I had been spring house cleaning - sorting out and re-packing clothes, washing windows, scrubbing the floor, all the usual house-cleaning chores. The creek was still frozen, and the ice on the river had not gone out yet.

We ran out of propane and it was too warm to fire up the big barrel cookstove in the kitchen. When Louis stopped later that day, I asked him to help me move the big barrel stove out and the old wood cookstove back in, holes and all, until we got more gas. I had to have something reasonable to cook on.

Chapter 15 Mary, Mary, How Does Your Garden Grow?

I t was that time of the year, almost spring, but not near enough yet and I was getting impatient to be getting my hands into the soil again and get the seeds and plants into the ground once more. We were going to plant everything we had in the way of seeds and plants, whether we could use it or not, to help fill our planting requirements. We had so much left to do, and only that summer to do it in. We wondered at that time if we would make it or not. The house looked like a jungle with plants everywhere. There were about 650 of them in all. If all the plants made it, we would have a prolific garden.

The creek finally opened up the first of May, and we were so happy to have water once more. Rapidly we became busy pulling out stumps and cutting up all the trees Mr. Rudder left laying around and clearing the rest of the ten acres for plowing. The stack of wood we had just from the old trees was immense. They were all old water-soaked cottonwoods, but we knew they would eventually all dry out and we could then burn them. Wally only cut the branches up and then used the small stuff to burn, and left the big trunks lay.

One weekend, when Clyde came home from Anchorage, the snow was gone, but the ground was still frozen, but the old grass was dry, and we thought it would be safe to burn it off so we could see what we had. Clyde cut a strip around the area we were to burn, and set it alight. The kids and I all stood by with buckets of water and soaked wet gunny sacks and it all burned well until it came to the big old crooked cottonwood tree in the front yard, and immediately caught the tree on fire, inside the tree. Try as we might, we couldn't put the fire out, and Clyde ran for the chainsaw, and proceeded to cut down the flaming tree. That was quite a feat, with the chainsaw full of gasoline, to cut down a fiercely burning huge old cottonwood. We had no idea the tree was dead, but it was all dry inside, and that was where the fire caught, just like a chimney, whoofing and burning rapidly. Once it was down, the fire went out. But it was very tricky, to say the least.

The ground was still too wet to plow and it was too cold at night to put out the plants. We hoped everything would be ready by the end of May, and we did have a good start, at least. I loved that time of year, with 20 hours of daylight once more, I felt so alive and energetic. And we were almost done with school once again.

The Gravely tractor Clyde had sent for arrived on Wednesday's freight, and since Clyde wasn't home, I unpacked the book of instructions and was trying to figure out how to start it to get it up to the house and into the shed, when Louis came by with Mabel and the boys. He started it for me and ran it up to the house too. We had a good visit, as usual. I knew I would miss them terribly when they moved.

When Clyde came home on the train Saturday, we really worked until 11 pm Saturday night. Clyde plowed all the old garden patches, and then about two acres in the field south of the house while I chopped the tops of the humps of roots with the adze, and the kids hauled rocks out of the field in their little red wagon. The tractor did a great job of plowing, even though I didn't think it was actually meant for use as a breaking plow. It was only a rotary garden plow, but it was the best we could afford. Even though it was slow going, we hoped to get the required plowing done on time.

Betty and Fred came up from town to clean up the yard around their cabin, just for the weekend. They brought their kids and a friend, Frank. They all came up to our house Sunday morning for coffee and gab. Fred and Frank shot a large black bear, and gave us the ribs for the dogs. When they caught the train later that day, Scotty and two friends from the army base in Fairbanks got off, and stayed in their cabin, but ate their meals at our house. That was the first day of the summer schedule for the train.

All day Sunday we plowed and worked, Sunday afternoon the Army boys came with a whole box full of ham, eggs, bacon, hot dogs, bread, juice, all yummy stuff, and had supper with us. I had baked four loaves of bread early Sunday morning and they ate three and a half of them! After supper they helped Clyde blow stumps out with dynamite, so things were really getting done faster, with help. Monday it rained and Clyde spent the time building a platform for our gas barrels. The freight left them off at Gold Creek by mistake, and Louis brought them down for us. We hauled them up in the cart that came with the tractor, and they were stored on the racks away from the house.

I baked six loaves of bread on Monday morning, and had to bake four more Tuesday. Clyde went back to town Monday and the boys went back to the base Tuesday. Bill wasn't with them, the Army sent him to Vietnam.

With all the food they brought, I really didn't mind cooking for them. They were a nice bunch of boys and really did hate the Army - and could they ever eat! They went through 14 loaves of my bread in the short time they were here. They came up to hunt but spent one whole afternoon helping Clyde dynamite stumps, and the kids took them on a tour of "their island" in the middle of the creek, all around their secret hide outs in the woods, down to the Susitna river and all over. They did see one bear and one moose, but only shot one porcupine and one squirrel, but we thought they really just came to get away from the Army base for a while. They planned to come back over the 4th of July weekend. The kids hoped that Pete would come back with them. He was a big clumsy fellow from Brooklyn, and a favorite with the kids. He actually fell in the creek after warning the kids not to fall in while he was crossing a log that they use as a bridge; the kids thought that was so funny they teased Pete all the time about it.

We planted potatoes the next weekend and after that was done we put out all the plants we had in the house. I already had transplanted nearly ¼ acre of strawberry plants and 21 new rhubarb plants, which were six inches high by that time. Everything was turning so pretty and green - still snow on the tops of the highest mountains, though.

While Clyde was working in Anchorage during the week, the kids and I continued hauling rocks and root clumps out of the fields to be plowed, and worked from sunup to sunset, practically, making things ready for Clyde to plow when he came home and each time he came home he broke a little more new ground with the rotary plow. As soon as I got used to driving the tractor with the cart attached, it became much easier for the kids and I to haul the wood from all the old logs and the big old crooked tree to the spot behind the house near where Clyde wanted to put the new and larger woodshed. Once we had that all cleared away, Clyde would be able to plow all that ground up as well. This whole place looked different with the big tree gone, and the stumps and logs all cut up and moved away. It was hard to believe how much it had changed; I really missed the old crooked tree.

Bud plowing the garden with the tiller   **Lisa in the cabbage patch**

Everything was planted the first seven days of June. All we had left to do as far as school was concerned was to box up all the books and mail them back to the school. Clyde got a few days off work so he could help us get everything planted. He plowed and we chopped and hauled. In each new strip of ground that was plowed we planted clover seed. The weather held hot and beautiful, and we worked as much as we could. It was very hard to see an end to all that work and sometimes we wondered if it was all worth it.

Mid-June came and it was our 12th anniversary and birthdays, and Clyde bought me a water pump, so no more hauling water by bucket! What a great gift that was. It ran with a gasoline motor and we had new hose all the way from the creek to the house. We had a big party to celebrate.

By the third week of June the potato plants were all up and everything else was too. The strawberries were all in bloom and making berries already. We had eaten several big desserts from the rhubarb patch already, and four wild rhubarb pies, besides the puddings. The wild rhubarb was good, milder than the domestic rhubarb, but by then it had all gone to seed and the stalks became too woody to eat.

We all had gorgeous suntans already that summer, and all of us enjoyed good health and the hot mosquito-free weather. When it was hot like that, the mosquitoes hid. We were gradually shoving back the wilderness, little by little. We thought, at that time, that we must have had about five acres plowed and cleared. Wishful thinking, I guess it was, but when we measured it out, we only had around two and a half acres done! How would we ever finish at that rate, on time?

The bridge crew was parked on the siding, a crew of three men and they all came up to the house for coffee a few times, and invited the kids and I down there for a spaghetti dinner they fixed, which was really good. They ran a big ditcher.

Louis and Mabel and the boys came down for dinner when Clyde was home once again and we had a party. Mabel caught us up on all the Gold Creek news, which was that Nellie had a houseful of company, and Mabel had gone fishing with Nellie's son Danny and Nancy, Nellie's daughter-in-law, whom I had yet to meet at that time. Nellie put all her visiting relatives to work on her garden, pulling every weed on the place. I could have used some help like that myself. The weeds grew faster than the plants and we had managed to keep all of them pulled, except out in the potato field, and it was just too big! We had to spend so much time cutting grass with the scythe and hand sickles, raking it into piles and hauling it away so that Clyde could plow each new patch of new ground when he came home. Oh, if only we had access to a bulldozer to clear the land fast by pushing all the trees and stumps into a pile, then we could have gotten all the land cleared in a hurry and met all the requirements on time. But there were no cats or equipment like that available, and to ship one up from any town would have cost a fortune for the freight alone both ways, not to mention the operator's pay. We had looked into that possibility; Clyde had asked around and called places to inquire, but no one was willing to rent out their equipment, and we could not borrow the amount of money it would have taken. We tried at the bank, but were told it wasn't possible, on our income or with our assets to get a loan large enough to do that.

And so we continued to work. Clyde planned to come home for a week or ten days as soon as he had enough annual and sick leave saved up so he could. Sometimes I was just so tired I could hardly move and I wondered if it was worth it all, but then after a good nights sleep and another sunny day, things always seemed better.

We all worked outside in shorts or bathing suits because it was too hot to wear heavier clothes. The kids were all in blooming good health, and grudgingly worked at whatever was required of them as long as they knew I would let them go 'swimming' in 'their' pond across the tracks.

The snow had been gone off the mountains since the 18th of June, and with all that rapid melting, the river and creek really filled up full. But the creek was back to normal, only a minor roaring torrent, and it left a nice little pool or pond across the tracks, on the north side of the creek, so the kids paddled around in that. They also had launched the old leaky wooden rowboat we had found in the weeds and paddled it around, while bailing furiously all the while. I sat in the shade nearby with the rifle, in case any bears came around. But none ventured near. The kids made such a racket it probably scared all the game in the general area away. I was certainly glad there weren't any neighbors for them to bother. They were always so happy to get back to 'freedom' after each trip to town, where they had to behave like 'civilized' people, and restrain their naturally exuberant natures.

I knew that John Glen and his two kids were coming up from Anchorage for the 4th of July, and also some of the boys from the Army base were expected from Fairbanks. I had no idea exactly how many people to expect, but since the days were still sunny and hot, the kids and I did some major house cleaning; hauling all the furniture out doors into the hot sunshine and threw buckets of water on the floor, scrubbed everything to within an inch of its life, beat and aired all the beds and the couch, and did a good job, too. We were all so hot and tired after we were all done, we all went down to the pond and jumped in to cool off. It was heavenly! Then I spent all morning on Friday, July 1st, baking bread and cakes.

It started clouding up about 2 pm Friday and sprinkling rain, of course, when the 4 pm train came from Fairbanks, and Scotty and Del got off. I was sort of surprised that we hadn't heard from them, and I wasn't sure they could make it after all. Of course, Scotty said I should have known he was coming because it was raining, naturally! After awhile we had dinner, and were so busy talking I missed the 7 pm Northwinds program. Scotty said he had mailed us a letter the Monday before, telling us that they were coming, and that two more guys were coming the next day, which was Saturday. We had not received the letter.

When the time for the next issue of Northwinds program came, I had the radio on and we all quieted down to listen. The first message was for me, sent by Clyde telling me he would be home sometime Friday evening. We didn't even have time to wonder how Clyde was getting home, when who should ride up through the potato field, right up to the back door, but Clyde! On his new shiny red Honda motorcycle, helmet and all! He had to get some means of transportation to work, and the cheapest he could find was the Honda, so he got it. Then he decided he could ride it up here instead of taking the train, and save train fare. It ran for 100 miles on a half-gallon of gas or less but he was one pooped guy, believe me! It took him eleven hours from Anchorage, by road to Talkeetna, and then by tracks from there home counting rest periods and eating time. At that time the Parks Highway, as it would be called later on, was gravel all the way from Wasilla, and not much better than a track in the wilderness from the Parks Highway to Talkeetna.

After Clyde ate something, we all talked a while longer, then we all went to bed. In about an hour and a half, I woke up because Clyde was screaming with cramps in both legs. Del slept through it all, but Scotty woke up and he knew what to do, thank heavens. Poor Clyde - his legs were one big mass of hard fist-sized knots. Scotty rubbed and pounded and I pulled and then put hot towels on until the cramps quit. But it took two hours. After that, Clyde went back to sleep and was okay, no more cramps. But he was still tired the next day.

Scotty and Del brought us twelve dozen eggs, six pounds of bacon, canned fruit, fresh peaches, and other goodies. They went up the mountain after bear Saturday morning, and when the train came at 1:15 pm, from Anchorage, John Glen and his two kids got off with the groceries Clyde had bought before he left town. Also, John brought four-dozen eggs, three pounds of coffee, two pounds of hot dogs, potato chips, and lot of other goodies.

We took pictures, went up to the house and ate lunch. Shortly thereafter, Scotty and Del came down off the mountain with no bear, tired and starving, and they ate also. Then it was time for the 4 PM train from Fairbanks, and Pete and Gary got off with potatoes, twelve pounds of hamburger, four-dozen eggs, salt, jam, and real butter. We had a real house full again. Betty and Fred didn't come at all that weekend.

I was not able to keep track of how much I cooked, but it seemed as if I was cooking all day and every day. At any rate, all the hamburger, hot dogs, potato chips, jam, ten dozen eggs, three pounds of coffee, fourteen loaves of my homemade bread, and six pounds of bacon were gone by the time everyone left on Monday, July 4th.

John helped Clyde most of the time, and so did Del, one day, cutting weeds and hauling rock out of the fields. John was a farmer at heart and Del was tired of hunting for nothing, so he stuck around and helped. John just wanted to come up and get away from the city and mess around in the garden a bit and fish a little. I really think he enjoyed himself. I know his kids sure liked it here a lot and our kids played really well together. They all had fun, and best of all, no fights.

It didn't rain too much during the days of that weekend, but it was cloudy all the time and sprinkled rain from time to time and rained hard in the late evenings some of the time, so the kids played outside a lot.

Scotty, Pete and Gary went Sunday afternoon on another hunt. They had been up the tracks, and up the mountain; that time they went down the tracks, looking for bear. They split up and found some sign, but no bear. On the way back, Scotty saw what he thought was a bear and shot it, but it was not a bear, it was a big bull moose, and was he ever pleased! He came home with a big grin all over his usually scowling face, until we lectured him royally about shooting that animal out of season and in mid-summer, of all things, with no refrigeration or anything. All he had done was to slit it's throat, and yelled for the other two, but none of them knew how to go about skinning an animal so large, and they came home for help. We were just sitting down to eat supper and they ate too, then all the men went back to skin out the moose. With six of them, it went pretty fast, and they carried the meat back in pack boards and a surgical tent brought for that purpose. We hung the quarters up in the partially done smokehouse, and put on a slow smoke to keep the flies away. Everyone had moose steaks and eggs for breakfast the next morning. I must have cooked at least 30 pounds of steak, and everyone loved the meat. It was tender and tasty. There weren't any leftovers. We even had fried potatoes with it.

The Army left for Fairbanks about 1:15 that day with about 50 pounds of meat all boxed up. John and his kids left for Anchorage about 4 PM with another 50 pounds or so of meat. It was cool enough to leave what was left here hang for a few days. We gave a quarter of it to Louis and Mabel, for their big freezer. Louis had a fit about them shooting a moose, but he realized that they were just Cheechakos after all, and had no idea how serious it could have been for them if they were caught, especially being in the Army. I salted and smoked a bunch of it, I didn't have time to can the meat, and Clyde took the rest of it to town when he left at the end of the week. He had taken the week off to try and get the plowing done, so of course it rained all week long and he hardly got any plowing done before the ground got too wet. Instead, we spent the week cutting and hauling wood, about 14 cords of it, and blowing up more stumps, built the woodshed and finished the smoke house, and re-fertilized the garden. That was after everyone left. When Clyde left, he took the train to town and shipped the motorcycle.

Our house certainly seemed big and roomy after everyone was gone. All the men were over six feet tall, and with all those big hulks in the house, it really seemed crowded. Actually, it was! Lisa slept in her box bed, made out of a large old wooden trunk with a mattress in it and the lid removed; Shelley and Debbie slept on the floor in sleeping bags in the bedroom. John's two kids slept on Debbie's bottom bunk bed; John slept on Shelley's bed; Del and Pete in their sleeping bags on the couch (it was a big couch); Scotty and Gary in their sleeping bags and air mattresses, which they brought, on the floor in the kitchen. Clyde and I slept in our own bed, and Bud in his. Sort of wall-to-wall people, so to speak. Definitely a full house. But we all had a good time and enjoyed having everyone here. I thought at that time that maybe we should open up a lodge.

One bad thing though, we all wished later that Gary had stayed in Fairbanks; He had a cold when he got here, and Monday night after everyone was gone, Lisa came down with it. Tuesday morning I had it; Tuesday night, Buddy, then Wednesday morning Shelley. Only Clyde and Debbie didn't catch it. We all loaded up on vitamins and got over the colds in good time, short but aggravating.

I was invited by the Army to come to Fairbanks, and they would show me the town. They said I could stay with Gary and his wife, who lived in a house off base. They all wanted me to teach Gary's wife how to bake bread (of all things!) They'd had such a good time, they wanted to give me a weekend on them, which I would have enjoyed, but never got to do because there was always too much to do around here. But it would have been fun.

I was so proud of the kids, they all worked like troopers, and our garden did wonderfully well that summer; we had wormless radishes, lettuce and turnip greens, new potatoes, carrots, turnips and beets. Even Louis praised the looks of our garden, on which we all worked very hard. I canned many jars of spinach greens mixed with turnip and mustard greens for the winter. The strawberries did fairly well also.

It was hot and dry with intermittent small showers for most of that summer. One day the temperature was 112 degrees in the sun, that lasted for three days, with 92 degrees in the shade, and the kids and I went swimming in what they called the "Big Pond", a slough (pronounced slew) by the river south of the house. The weather had been so hot that the water was almost warm. The woods became so dry they announced over the radio for no one to burn brush or trash until another general soaking rain.

Debbie & Lisa swimming in the Slough

The heat was hard on the dogs as well, even though we had them tied out in the shady woods where it was coolest. They hardly barked at all when anyone came around, just lay under a cool log and panted. We took Yukon swimming with us one day, he really liked it. There were no bears around anywhere; they were all up in the hills cooling off.

Chapter 16 Bureaucratic Frustrations

C lyde went to the Land Bureau and tried to apply for an extension of time, but they weren't giving any extensions anymore, we guessed because the State had taken all the land around our claim. They told him that if he wanted to give back eighty acres, all he had to have plowed and planted was five acres by August 12th, and keep it plowed and planted until it was inspected for approval. If not done by then, we had to have ten acres plowed and planted by the next August 12th, to keep the eighty acres, or twenty acres done for the whole 160 acres we had filed upon. What an ultimatum that was! We had already worked ourselves almost to death to get the little bit we did have cleared and plowed. What would we ever do?? If we decided to give up 80 acres, it would have to be the mountain we gave up, since we lived on the flat, but we hated to think of giving up any of it. We didn't know what to do. This all came about in the middle of July. We thought we had over three acres done, that is, plowed and planted, and had brushed and burned off another two or three acres and the kids and I had hauled out deadfalls and branches and stumps while Clyde was in town working, so that when he came home he could plow it and we could plant it right behind him. Oh how we yearned for a bulldozer or some easy way to get it all done. It took so very much time doing all that by hand. The Alaska homestead laws were really very unfair, since we had such short summers in which to accomplish anything. They were really the old Kansas homestead laws and it seemed like the Bureau of Land Management tried to make things as hard for the homesteader as possible. The State had taken over all the land around our place, and even wrote us a letter stating that if we didn't intend to do anything with our place, it would become State property also, which panicked us, for sure.

As soon as the sun went behind the mountain around 8:30 PM, all the mosquitoes came roaring out of hiding like a battalion of bombers, and zeroed in for the kill. Though it didn't get dark the temperature dropped about 10 degrees. It was quite dusky about 11 pm until about 1 am or so when the sun came up from behind the mountain once again. The glaciers were melting in all that heat and the Susitna River was almost as full as it was the summer before, with all the rain there was that summer, and very silty. The fish report on the radio said that the red, silver and pink salmon were just starting up the mouth of the Susitna, down below Anchorage and I knew it wouldn't be long before we had good fishing once again here. The fish report also said that there was such a good run of salmon that the canneries were all over loaded and couldn't handle them all. The Japanese had three freezer ships standing by to take on the excess. It was certainly a good year for everything.

There were dozens of different kinds of birds around; perhaps because of all the insects and new soil turned over, it seemed to attract many of them. Of the ones I recognized there were robins, starlings, wrens, magpies, chickadees, skylarks and the little ones we called snowbirds, chickadees and camp robbers. There were many birds I had never seen before, but it sounded so nice to hear the chirping and twittering in the early mornings. There was one camp robber living near here that ate out of our hands. Every morning we went out and there he was, waiting for a handout. We always gave him a crust of bread or biscuit, or a chunk of dog food, and once he even sat on Bud's hand to eat. What a thrill that was for him, and for us to watch, as well. The camp robber took what we gave him and flew off with it in his beak, and came back when he felt like it later in the day. Most of them seemed very tame. But only that one would eat out of our hands.

A porcupine was chewing on the corner of the house, and when Clyde tried to chase it away, it headed for the dogs; no matter how it was shoved and turned around, it kept heading for the dogs, so Clyde shot it. We gave the ribs to the dogs, and cooked the legs fried nice and brown and then simmered for a while in gravy, with carrots, onions and new potatoes from our garden. It was a delicious "porky" stew, with a salad of lettuce, radishes and green onions, and a big bowl of sliced raw turnips as well. I still thought porcupine tasted a little like rabbit, I was never quite sure. We didn't see any more the rest of that summer.

We had only twenty-two days left to finish our requirements, if we decided to go for the five acres cleared in order to keep 80 acres and give up the other eighty. We worked and worked and finally, with only eleven days left to the deadline, we thought we had finally finished plowing and planting five full acres. We planted clover seed where nothing else was planted, to meet the requirements. We measured, and re-measured yet again to be sure and the numbers seemed to come out right.

After much discussion and figuring out every way possible, and after Clyde did some extensive calling around town, yet again pricing things, we decided we would have to give up the eighty acres and go for clearing just the five acres. JUST!! What a laugh, and what a monumental task that was! We re-set our back boundary posts, and then Clyde went in to file.

Reluctantly we gave up our eighty acres of mountain, kept our eighty acres of valley, and Clyde paid the final closing costs when he filed the final proof. We were all exhausted after working so hard. We had to keep those five acres plowed and planted until someone from the land office came out to inspect and measure it all.

Meanwhile, about August 1st that summer, which was a very hot day, Bill from the Gold Creek section stopped in and told us there were pink salmon in the creek mouths just south of us, and the kids and I thought we had better check out our own creek. Of course Clyde had the fishing poles and nets and tackle in town, so we made a net out of a gunnysack and some stiff wire, and I brought along the rifle in case of bear. When we got down to the river and the mouth of our creek we were astounded to see so many salmon. There were at least thirty of them resting in the mouth of the creek and swimming around in the creek clear up to where the woods started. We tried and tried to catch them in the 'net', but couldn't do so, and in desperation I shot three of them, and the kids waded in and grabbed them, and we cleaned them there. Then it started to rain, so we came home and had our lovely delicious pink salmon rolled in corn-meal and fried to a crisp golden brown with a big pan of corn bread and a big bowl of salad and tartar sauce. Oh, but they were good!

The run of salmon that year set a record over any other year, to date, according to the fish and game report on the radio. The fishermen were all getting rich. Each and every day they were catching as many as their boats or nets would hold, and no limit was set, since the Japanese freezer ships came to buy the excess. At first the canneries couldn't handle them all, and they had to limit each fisherman to 600 fish a day for three days until the Japanese ships arrived. The Governor sent for them, actually. At that time there were ten freezer ships and each could take 50,000 pounds of fish a day. Our canneries, of course came first, and were taking all the fish they could possibly handle.

The fish and game people allowed the fishermen to fish seven days a week, twenty-four hours a day, that's how good the run of salmon was. The reds and kings were in first; they estimated from the air over ten million fish in each school, and two or three schools a day, mostly reds. The kings were still only about one-third strength at that time, with a heavy king run only every seven years.

The red salmon run lasted about ten days, school after school of fish and lots of escapement with that many fish. Then came pinks and silvers and last of all chums, in runs of varying sizes, but millions of them. It had been about a week before that time that the report had come on the radio they were spotted starting up the mouth of the Susitna River. I thought the fish had arrived shortly before we went down to the creek mouth. It was certainly something to see – all those fins in OUR creek, and out on the river there must have been hundreds of thousands of them making their way north to their spawning grounds.

The red salmon run around Seward, Kenai and Anchorage was about over but the pinks were still coming on strong.

I wrote to Clyde and asked him to send quickly, some nets and the pole and snag hooks because I wanted to catch as many of those fish as possible, I needed to can as much as I could and smoke and dry some as well. I remembered that the last summer, the Salmon runs were so poor, fisherman were limited to seven or eight hours of fishing, and only three or four days a week, to allow for escapement. The difference in the two years was astounding.

We were kept very busy with the fish and all that entailed for about ten days or so, and when Clyde came home, of course, he helped us and we all had fish coming out our ears, so to speak. The more ragged fish we hung on racks to dry and kept a slow smoke on them;

they were used to supplement the dogs' food. By that time we had several hundred fish on the drying/smoking racks under a tarp roof.

We noted the water in the creek was tasting 'fishy' and spent the better part of a day clamoring among the rocks with gunny sacks, picking dead fish out of the bushes where they had become stranded when the water level went down in the creek. So all up and down our creek it seemed, the fish were spawning. We had been told by Dixie and Wally there never were any fish in the creek! If they had seen it then, they probably would not have believed it. We carried gunnysacks full of dead fish home and buried them in the rhubarb and strawberry patches for fertilizer. This was later in the month, after the run was all over. Shortly thereafter it rained in torrents and washed the creek clean. For a short time we had been forced to get our water from the spring, which was farther from the house, but had no fish in it.

Mabel, Louis and the boys were all on the train near the end of August. It was time for Louis' vacation and he was spending it moving Mabel and the boys to a house in town so their oldest boy could go to school. I didn't even have the chance to see Mabel and say goodbye. But Louis came back for a few months until he was transferred in January, 1967, to Girdwood section, South of Anchorage. We missed them all.

Then Johnny, the track patrolman left for his month long vacation. He bought round trip airline tickets for two friends of his in Australia to come to Alaska and spend their vacation with him. He planned to take them all around Alaska and did. He drove them on every available road, from Seward to Fairbanks and points between, then on the train to several cabins where they camped out. I met them on the train when I went to town. They had so much to tell all their friends when they got back to Australia. They were a nice couple.

Our vegetables were king-size and beautiful. I canned everything, and even made a small batch of sauerkraut, just to see how it would turn out. I had never tried making it before, but found a great recipe for it in my Ball canning book, the book that came with my new pressure canner. I used that wonderful little book till it fell apart; it was my lifesaver as far as canning went.

We dug about 70 lbs of new potatoes in about 20 minutes one day, great big potatoes, and we only dug up every third plant in two short rows.

According to the gardening guide I had obtained from the Extension Service in Anchorage, in order to get white cauliflower I had to tie the leaves up to cover the white part. I did that and it worked. We had big beautiful white heads, full and tight and delicious. I tried pickling some and it turned out well, also pickled some beets. I was certainly getting a liberal education with all these new things to learn and try.

We had not been out picking currents, as yet, since it rained non-stop for about ten days. But that gave me a chance to catch up on all the canning and other things I had been neglecting. When the rain stopped and the bushes dried out a bit, we went out, armed with buckets and the gun, and picked and picked. The cranberries were not quite all red as yet, but they were coming right along.

So far we had not had frost; we were expecting it at any time. The temperature had been down to 39 degrees one night, and all my tomato and cucumber plants died, without making anything. They were a waste of time and effort without a greenhouse to put them in.

Lisa in the corn 1960's

We had a fair yield of summer squash, and I made a big pan of it steamed with butter; the kids all loved it that way. The cabbages were really huge. After last summer, we could hardly believe how big everything was; baseball sized turnips and the carrots were large, crisp and delicious. The beets were very big as well, and very good. Everything was lush.

We planted clover on all the land we had cleared and plowed that didn't have vegetables planted to meet our requirements. Clyde re-measured the entire place and came up with almost seven acres cleared, plowed and planted, including where the house sits, the regular garden, strawberry and rhubarb patches.

Clyde filed our final proof at the land office on August 12, the deadline date, and paid all the fees. They told him that all we had to do was wait for the inspectors to come out and measure and approve our plowing, but until that happened, we had to keep all of it plowed, and planted. They could give him no idea when that might be. They told him that after the inspection, if it was approved, then the surveyors would come out and survey our 80 acres, and after that we would get our patent, or deed. We had worked every day, rain or shine, to get it all done, and barely in time.

It was September 8 again, two years exactly since we had moved on to this place. Time certainly did fly by; everything was so different. It frosted only two days before and we started digging potatoes, and would be digging them for a while.

Then I got sick, and had to go to town to see a doctor. It was only a kidney infection and I got better in a hurry with the medicine the doctor gave me. Clyde was at home with the kids. While in town I saw Betty and Fred and they said they were not coming up to live that winter. They expected to come up and spend Christmas and stay only through New Years. I was disappointed, to say the least. I had been counting on neighbors again, since all my new friends at Gold Creek seemed to be deserting. Nellie was moving to Kenai, and Mabel and Louis and family were gone.

I had a terrible feeling it was going to be a fierce winter. Everything was too lush all summer. The wild animals were fat, and had thick coats already; a bad sign, the old-timers said. We had done all we could do to prepare for a really tough winter. Our shelves were stuffed full of canned goods from the garden; there were gunnysacks full of potatoes under every bed; the woodshed was full of split wood stacked neatly waiting.

As soon as Clyde finished insulating the cellar we sorted the potatoes and stored them down where it was cool enough to keep them, we hoped.

School started once again at Sherman. Then, of course, Scotty came back for one final try for his bear. He came for a week, and Clyde stayed home to hunt with him.

The next morning early, Bud, Scotty and Clyde went up in the mountains behind the house looking, and Scotty shot a caribou. They explored five miles back through tundra country up on top of the mountains. They left here before 8 am, and didn't get back until 11 PM. I was terribly worried, and about ready to call out a rescue squad or something. It was very dark, but they made it all right. They had no flashlights with them, not expecting to be gone that long. Another lesson learned by all – be prepared. They were exhausted almost to the point of being ill. The next night we had the most outrageous display of northern lights we had ever seen. All colors, all shapes, from a huge cone over the top of the house to waving ribbons of light, and rays slanting up from the hilltops. Almost too much to take in all at once, It was a grand show.

Two days later Scotty finally got his bear, a nice fat black bear. I had to show him how to skin it out with the head and feet attached so he could send it off to have a wall mount rug made. He left most of the meat here for us, and left happy with his longed-for bear hide and some meat, and we never saw him again. He did send a post card from time to time, but over the years we lost track of him. Bill sent letters from Vietnam but after he went home we seldom heard from him, either, except for a Christmas card a few times. But we remember them all, and hope they are all well and happy.

Louis was back from his vacation and he came by to tell us Nellie and Nancy (Nellie's daughter-in-law) were up in Gold Creek digging Nellie's potatoes and that Nellie wanted to see me on Monday if I could make it. I told Louis to tell her we would be there for sure, and around noon Monday Louis came in his gas car and picked us up. He dropped us off at Nellie's path and when we got to her house it was locked and nobody was around. So the kids and I followed a back road for a mile or so around the woods and didn't seem to get anywhere. I really had no idea where Nancy's cabin was, and so decided to head back to the section house, before we got lost. We were there for about half an hour when Louis came and I told him what had happened. He took us back and showed me how to find Nancy's cabin. It was a good mile back in the woods along a road that branched off the end of Nellie's airstrip. Sure enough, when we got there, there was Nellie up on the roof nailing back a piece of metal roofing that had blown off during the wind storm Sunday night, and Nancy was cutting wood with a little chain saw. They thought we would hear all the noise they were making and be able to find the cabin. But we hadn't heard a thing until the cabin was actually in sight, and they hadn't heard us shouting, either. We had a grand visit, and I was so glad to finally get to meet Nancy. She was a short bouncy cute gal with two adorable kids, a boy of four and a girl, five and Nancy was really nice, too. We hit it off right away and have been fast friends now, for over 38 years.

Mary, Shelley, Beth (Mary's sister) & Debbie-got ourselves a 'bar'

I loved her cabin, made of logs. It was new and still had the white look of freshly peeled logs, and of course they had lots of pretty furniture and it was just fixed up beautifully. It was bigger than Nellie's cabin, but one story with a log beam ceiling. Nancy said she would be spending the winter there, she thought, but Nellie was planning to spend the winter in Kenai with her husband, John. Nellie told me my garden did better than hers and she was proud of me. She told me what, when and how to plant to get the best results, and since I followed her directions, and they worked, we were both pleased. Nellie also sold me her wonderful treadle model sewing machine she had bought new from

Sears about 25 years before. It worked beautifully and still does to this day.

About 6 pm we left to walk back to the section house. Nancy and her daughter Noelle came with us because she wanted to see Louis about something, she said, but I thought she probably wanted to make sure we did not get lost. Louis could not take us home until after 7:30 since a freight train was on the tracks and he had to wait for them to pass by. It was raining by then, too, though it had not been raining before.

The rest of the week we spent doing school and banking up the outside of the house with dirt to keep the worst of the cold at bay when it came. We had aluminum panels all around the bottom of the house, and rocks piled up in front of them so it didn't take as much dirt, but we had to pile it to floor level. We spent a few hours each afternoon, after the ground thawed a bit doing that.

Then when it was wood hauling time, to make it more fun, we harnessed Yukon to a small sled and let him pull it over the ground the short distance to a wood pile and tied on two small cottonwood logs and he dragged them back to the house. We knew it would be easier in the snow, but people recommended starting training on bare ground if possible. He did just great. He was about six and a half months by then, weighed about 60 pounds and was floppy eared and clumsy but speedy in spite of himself.

When November came, Shelley went to Anchorage for an eye operation that had been scheduled for some time. She had been wearing corrective glasses and an eye patch to strengthen her 'bad' eye, and the doctor felt it was time. Her operation was a big success, and she did not even have to wear glasses for some time afterwards.

It was 10 degrees below zero, and in order to keep the temperature warm enough in the cellar, we burned a kerosene storm lantern down there and it kept the air around 35 to 40 degrees. We hoped that would be warm enough to keep the potatoes from freezing. We had eight inches of snow by that time, and the wind had been blowing most of the time, making it colder than ever.

Every time Clyde came home we had to box up or bag up more potatoes because he kept having requests from folks he worked with to bring them some. It was a good thing folks wanted to buy them, because we had over 1500 pounds in the cellar already, and that was quite a bit more than we needed. I estimated that Clyde had given away and/or sold over eight hundred pounds of them, and we had about two to three hundred pounds bagged up and ready for future customers.

The river was already frozen clear across and all jammed with big blocks of ice. Every day we had to chop through about six inches or more of ice to get water out of the creek. If it hadn't snowed the little bit it did, the creek would have been frozen dry. Part of the woodshed roof blew off. Nothing was damaged and when Clyde came home the next weekend he fixed that roof.

Where the Susitna river flows past Curry it becomes very narrow and the chunks of ice were stacked eight to twelve feet in the air and there along the banks were massive piles of it, also near here. We were afraid the ice would come clear up to Betty and Fred's cabin when spring break up happened.

Louis came over for 'early' Thanksgiving dinner, because Clyde wasn't able to take off work for the week in order to stay home for the holiday. We had much to be thankful for, and decided to have our Thanksgiving with the whole family together. We had turkey with oyster and giblet dressing, candied sweet potatoes, French cut green beans seasoned with chunks of ham, corn on the cob, mashed potatoes and turkey gravy, hot yeast rolls, cranberry sauce, olives and pickles, pumpkin pies and whipped cream and a chocolate cream pie, just for Louis.

We all ate until we could not hold any more! We had a very nice time and I think Louis enjoyed it too, even though Mabel and the boys were not there. We all missed them so much.

The moose were scarce and we did not see one at all. But Louis shot two caribou, across the creek, and gave us part of the meat.

Chapter 17   Goodbye To A Faithful Friend

That winter whenever we hitched the dogs up to work, Johnnie would growl ferociously at Copper, and finally one day he attacked Copper and they fought fiercely. It was all Clyde could do to get them apart without being injured himself. So from then on we only put Johnnie on line with Yukon. By then Yukon was eight months old, but he was bigger than either Johnnie or Copper and strong. Copper was the best natured of them all and friendly with strangers also. We talked the situation over as a family, letting the children help us decide what to do and agreed that we would have to find another home for Johnnie, who wasn't as much of a 'Teddy Bear' as he used to be. Clyde and I were afraid that one of the kids would be hurt, or even bitten. Johnnie had become just too possessive of us all, and even attacked the lineman one day, whom he had known since he was a small puppy. He broke his chain and rushed down the path as Tony was coming up the path to the house, and bit him on the arm. Fortunately Tony was wearing a big bulky down filled parka and no harm was actually done to his arm. But the potential was there, and we could not have a biting dog around the kids.

Later on that winter we gave Johnnie to a professional dog musher, and Johnnie lived out his years doing what he liked best, running and pulling a sled. We saw him once more, and he seemed happy to see us but also happy in his new home. We decided to keep Copper as an all around pet and work dog and found a home for Yukon as well, with two old ladies in Anchorage, who needed a watch dog. Yukon was a splendid one, and lived happily there in his new home as well.

Bud Lovel & Copper

We decided to buy a snow machine – thought it would be less trouble than dogs, and wouldn't need to be fed all summer while not working either.

Clyde with the Polaris snow machine

As far as school went that year, I was ready to tear out my hair and send the whole mess back. The courses had all been changed and they were complicated and confusing. The "New Math" had been inserted and no matter how much I studied the teacher's manual, I could not understand it at all, and it only served to confuse the kids, who were used to standard math. From what I understood, the teachers in Anchorage were having the same problems. Most of them had to go to school for refresher courses or in the case of the modern math, a whole three months to learn how to do it, and how to teach it. I finally deciphered the rest of the lessons and in desperation I wrote a letter to the Correspondence Study program teachers and objected to the modern math and explained all the difficulties we were having. The head of the program wrote back to me that I could exchange those books for standard math books once again, and I jumped at the chance. From then on, we made it okay.

Around the end of November we had a Chinook. We had been out hauling wood and ice with the dogs until it got too warm to work the dogs any more. The Chinook had begun to blow and the temperature soared to 42 degrees above zero and stayed there for three hours. It was so warm we let the barrel stove go out altogether, cleaned all the ashes out of it and hauled them away. We kept a small fire in the kitchen range until the temperature went back to 35 degrees, when it became dark. All night it was warm, only getting down to 28 degrees, which seemed warm to us after days of below zero weather. Before it had turned so cold, it snowed non-stop until the accumulation was two more feet on top of the old snow. The moose began to come down out of the hills.

Louis brought down some old light gray paint he didn't need or want, and since it was warm enough to open the windows, I got to work painting the kitchen ceiling. It was an open beam ceiling, and blackened from years of smoke, and ugly. I thought a coat or two of paint would lighten up the place and perhaps make it look better, though there wasn't really much one could do to make that old cabin look less like a sows ear, so to speak. But I found that one coat hardly made any difference at all. That old wood just soaked it up like a sponge, and I knew it would take at least two or three more coats of paint to even begin to make a difference. But the Chinook stopped blowing and I had to stop painting because it was too cold to keep the windows open, and the fumes were too much.

About mid-December I sent the kids in with Clyde so they could spend their 'allowances' on Christmas presents, and I stayed home to keep the lantern in the cellar going, and the house warm enough so none of the hundreds of jars of canned goods would freeze. Since everyone was gone I took advantage of the peace and quiet and time, and finished painting the kitchen. Also managed to answer the reams and reams of mail waiting to be answered. Clyde saw to it before they left that I had plenty of ice stacked up in boxes and buckets for water and plenty of wood close to the door so I wouldn't have to do any of those chores myself. I had to put white on the ceiling before it would take the light gray paint, and it certainly did lighten it up in there. The walls I painted white, as well. Also painted the table, benches and wood box dark gray with light gray top on the table and wood box. It looked bright and clean and nicer than it did.

The old heavy chainsaw broke down before Clyde left and he took it to town with him to get parts or have it repaired. But it would be so long before it could be repaired that he had to buy a new one, in order to keep up with the woodcutting.

I caught the 4am train on Thursday to join the family in town only to be met at the station with the news that Debbie had the mumps! Our luck was holding, it seemed. Her fever was down and she felt pretty good except for the lumps on her neck. Keeping her quiet was quite a job but we managed with color books and things. But all I got done was to buy a little groceries, a few clothes the kids and I needed really bad, and a few little things for the kids for Christmas. I only had the one day to shop, and the day I arrived, actually, which was Friday, and then Saturday Clyde and I and Bud and Lisa came home with the new chain saw. We left Shelly in town to stay with Debbie for the weekend so she wouldn't feel so abandoned. John was kind enough to keep the two kids for us.

On the train, I met another of our neighbors, Sandy Couty, one of the Erickson's daughters. She was married to Doug, and lived in Chulitna, some 14 miles north of Gold Creek. Her house was on the other side of a lake from the railroad tracks, and it was one half mile by dog sled across the lake or one and one tenth mile around the lake. They had a generator and indoor plumbing and all, even a telephone, but that was in a little green box nailed to a spruce tree near the railroad tracks. We had a really nice visit, and she told us she had two little boys, age one and a half and three and a half, and her husband ran a trap line with the five dogs they had in the winter, and worked at construction summers. Of course Clyde had met her and seen her several times on the train since he took it almost every weekend but it made the trip seem shorter to have a woman to talk to. There were so few around here! I had seen Betty in town – she was working four nights a week at a Pizza place and Fred was not working at that time.

It started snowing before we got back from town and warmed up and was snowing when we got home and snowed about eight inches worth and the moose were down from the hills at last.

Louis came down with a box of moose ribs (from a carcass the train hit way up north) for dog food and bait for Bud's traps and he said that Mabel and the boys might be up for Christmas week. We hoped so.

Clyde went back to town Sunday, the next day, and planned to return the next Saturday with the girls, which would be the weekend before Christmas Eve. Debbie was fine, and I suspected that Lisa would probably get the mumps around Christmas or New Years, since she was the only child left who had not had the mumps as yet. Clyde was taking the entire week off for Christmas and planned to spend most of it cutting more wood. He had to go back though on New Years Day but would have the day after New Years off work to rest up from the week at home.

Christmas week it snowed all week, and had warmed up to 30 degrees. We had a very nice Christmas, but did not get to see Mabel and the boys, since every one of them were sick and had not come up to Gold Creek after all. Our families sent the usual and very welcome 'care' packages along with Christmas presents for all. Also 'dinner on us' boxes and everything was enjoyed immensely. Our 'big' present to Bud was his very own single shot .410 shotgun, which he was only allowed to use when with one of us. Never alone, at least until he was older. He was thrilled, of course.

My mother wrote that they were planning to come up sometime in the summer of 1967, and I was ecstatic, to finally be able to see my family again! I wrote back immediately telling them of what happened in which summer months, and they finally decided to drive up, and bring Grandma and my two youngest brothers, pulling a travel trailer. We had that to look forward to all the rest of the winter, and until they actually arrived from California in August of that year.

We still had plenty of wood in the woodshed and stacked up on the south side of the porch, but it had been cold enough to be cautious about the wood supply. The coldest it had been so far that winter was minus 34 degrees, which was cold enough for anyone. It had not lasted very long, but we knew it could get colder, and in fact it did. The new chain saw worked very well, and was even light enough that I could use it, and also Bud, if necessary. All Christmas week the temperatures stayed warm, from 21 degrees above zero to 31 degrees, and we were grateful.

Clyde spent the week strengthening the woodshed roof, cutting more wood, and he and Bud tried to run the dogs when it wasn't snowing too hard, but the going was rough in the soft snow. Clyde replaced a bad section of stove pipe with new pipe, cleaned the chimneys, shoveled snow off the roofs and paths, and I had a chance to catch up on sewing and mending, and also took apart and cleaned the cook stove. Then we painted the floor and kitchen pantry shelves.

When the weather cleared up it returned to zero and then to five below zero. It was cold enough to run the dogs and Bud and I tried it.

144

The snow had been too soft while it was warmer but we snow shoed the trails first which made it easier for the dogs to pull the sled. By that time we had more than five feet of snow on the ground and my muscles were sore from the first time that year on snowshoes. I read somewhere that those particular muscles were not used very much except when snow shoeing. I also knew (from the winter before) that only the first time made me sore, and did not bother me any more after that.

We enjoyed the sunrise/sunset glow during the lightest part of the days in the south end of our valley and were looking forward to actually seeing the sun once again.

The dogs were barking frantically and I looked out the window to see a lovely lynx cat nose to nose with Johnnie. It was standing very still and letting Johnnie sniff and snarl at it. So I grabbed the 22 rifle and ran out the door and spoke softly to Johnnie so he would see the gun (he was very gun shy) and he dived into his doghouse, out of the way. The lynx looked skinny and only moved an inch or so, but turned and snarled at me when I fired off a shot in the air to try to scare it away. So I shot it. It was a female, and had a lovely pelt, and we took pictures before I skinned her out. She measured just over five feet in length stretched out, bigger than I thought lynx were and that, to date (it was February by then) was the largest game I had ever shot. Not knowing much about the habits of a lynx, I had no idea why she was so near the dogs, but I saw that the claws and teeth were deadly, and felt I would rather shoot the cat than have to shoot a mauled dog. I thought she was trying to attack Johnnie, actually. She was very thin and probably starving.

A few days before that the dogs were all howling, and we thought a freight train was coming, so didn't pay any attention. When we finished school for the day, we hitched up Johnnie and Bud rode on the sled to the woodpile, about a quarter mile south of the house. I gave the other two dogs a biscuit to shut them up, but even while they were munching, I heard howling sort of north and east coming from the base of the mountains behind the house. There were three or four wolves howling and snarling, it sounded like, and that is what our dogs had been doing, answering them. We never saw those wolves, only heard them howling for about an hour. That was one of the reasons why we kept our dogs chained most of the time. Since they were huskies, there was enough of the wolf strain in them to possibly make them run off to join a wolf pack and probably get killed in the process. One never knew what to expect next living in the wilderness. It tended to keep life interesting.

By March we had another three feet of snow, practically burying the house. I estimated we had a good six feet of packed snow. We have to go up a packed hill to get to the path, and from the north we can walk right up a snow bank and onto the woodshed roof, only a foot above. Every time it snows we take turns snow shoeing the paths to the outhouse, woodshed, mailbox down by the tracks, and to the creek where we chopped ice for our drinking water.

Clyde put up a mail box down by the tracks so that whoever was running the tracks, when they went by and saw the red flag up on the mailbox and the red rag hanging on a stick, they would know we had mail to go. Since Louis was gone for good, having been transferred to Girdwood section, our mail did not get delivered or picked up unless we let someone know. And so we made those arrangements with Leroy, the new track patrolman from Curry, and before too long, the conductors on the passenger trains started throwing off our incoming mail as they went by, with a rock in the sack to keep it from blowing away, and only if one of us was out there waiting. They were very good about it.

Clyde sent us a Northwinds message to meet the freight one night. It was not the regular 'Peddler', but a through freight, as, the message said, he sent a package for us with the conductor of that freight. So Bud and I put on our snowshoes when we heard the freight whistle, and carrying a storm lantern each, snow shoed our way down to the tracks to wait. It was only about 30 degrees above zero and snowing, and while we were waiting we got busy shoveling the five foot heap of snow the rail road snow plow had shoved on to our bridge which also had buried the mailbox, so we could get to the tracks. When we were finished, we put a lantern on the snow bank on each side of the path we had made, and sat down to wait. Pretty soon we heard a gas car from the north, and it sounded like it was having motor trouble. Every few minutes we heard it quit, and a bunch of banging around, and a man shouting. This went on for ten or fifteen minutes, and finally we saw the light and the gas car was almost to the bridge over the creek when two moose came into view. Well, there we were, no gun, in the dark, and there came the two moose heading straight down the center of the tracks right for us, ahead of the gas car. All we could do was hide behind the snow bank and watch, because we could not run – (our snowshoes were off) and the moose both paused not more than ten feet from us and looked at our lanterns and then trotted on. The gas car stopped, and the patrolman got out and asked us if we heard the freight yet and we told him what we had heard. He said he had been having engine trouble for the last 20 miles and to top it off had to chase those two moose all the way from above Gold Creek, and they wouldn't leave him alone and he had no gun! He was so mad he was about to burst because railroad regulations would not allow guns on patrol cars. I thought that was rather dangerous for the men running the cars. He said most of the men carried guns for their own protection but if they were caught at it, they would be fired. He radioed ahead to see where the train was and went on to park and wait at the Sherman siding. So Bud and I went back home and when we were positive we heard the freight, then we went back down to the tracks with the gun. But the freight was not chasing any moose, and they slowed down and the engineer threw off the package, and asked how we all were doing, we told him we were all fine, and then the train went on.

The next night a pickup truck on rail wheels stopped and shone a spotlight in the windows to get our attention. I went out and was heading toward the tracks when a man yelled that they had just shot a moose a 'little ways' on the other side of our creek, right next to the tracks, if we wanted it. Did we ever! We had been longing for fresh meat for several months by that time.

Bud and I went out with a gun, two storm lanterns, an axe, three knives, shovels and snowshoes. We walked and walked and over one third mile later, closer to half a mile actually, finally found the moose. We cut it open and out came a she calf (what a shame – the cow had a broken leg) We had it all gutted and half skinned when the men came back in a gas car, about 10 PM. They decided they had better help us because there was a train due at 1:30 am, and it wouldn't be so good to be seen with a fresh carcass (especially a cow) at this time of year. So they chopped off the head and cut the carcass in two across the backbone and dragged half at a time (hair side down) to our path behind the gas car. We got it all up to the house by 11 PM, but it took Buddy and I until 2 am to finish skinning it and cutting it in quarters to hang up. We were exhausted! Buddy is a strong and energetic little boy at 10 years old, not so little really, and doing a man's job. I was proud of him.

The next day we feasted on steaks – tender and juicy. We certainly needed that meat. God did provide, and the railroad helped too.

We had a code worked out in case I got a moose when Clyde was gone. It went like this: "Emergency supplies arrived finally – feeling better so don't send the doctor. Bring home shelf paper without fail, and check on outside part of axe grinder." Meaning – "Got a moose, so don't buy any meat to bring home – or dog food – also bring freezer paper to wrap meat in, and the big meat grinder." Simple. Since I was too tired the next day to walk down to the dispatch phone in the little booth by the siding, when the new Gold Creek foreman stopped that morning, (just to ask if I shot a moose the night before) because there was a trail of blood all down the tracks and up our path where the moose was dragged. When I told him no, I hadn't shot a moose, he asked Buddy laughingly if he'd had a nosebleed. I told him two men had stopped and told us they had to shoot it because it had a broken leg and wouldn't get off the tracks, and the foreman said, "Yeah, right. Who were those men?" I told him I had no idea, because it was dark when they stopped. Of course I knew who those men were, but I didn't know this man and was afraid he would turn us all in. But I asked him if he would call Clyde and give him the code message, and reverse the charges. I'm sure the foreman thought I was insane, but it was a regular telephone, a 10 party line, at the section house and I thought it best to use the code. Just in case; Bud and I got busy right away and managed to completely cover up the evidence as soon as possible as soon as the foreman went on. Buddy and I had buried the head and entrails and blood at the site itself but it didn't occur to us about the clear and very red trail from there to the house.

Several days later, the new foreman stopped again and let his stepdaughter off for a visit and to meet us. She was just a year or two older than Shelley. Her name was Norma and she was a cute little Eskimo girl of 13, and bored to tears with life in Gold Creek. Her schoolbooks had not arrived yet, and she had virtually 'nothing to do'. She was a real 'city kid' and shy at first, but didn't have a chance of staying that way with our kids' boisterous and outgoing natures. I was glad that Shelley finally had a girl near her own age at last and they became good friends. Norma came back whenever her step dad had to work down this way, and time allowed.

In those days we still had airmail, and even airmail letters sometimes took 20 days or more to get to us. It was frustrating, but a fact of life at that time. Regular mail took from two weeks to a month or more, depending on where it got mis-sent, and to what remote village somewhere. I have wondered through the years if we actually got all our mail or if some was lost forever in the great void. But on the other end of the scale, sometimes regular mail only took three to five days to reach us. It was amazing. I would get a letter from my mother asking if I had received the letter telling me about something, and then a week later I would get the letter in question, or not get it at all.

When Clyde came home that weekend he said there were dead moose all over the place, having been hit by the trains, and sometimes along the roads, even by cars. It seemed the deep snow made the moose stick to roads and paths and plowed places, like the railroad tracks. He said there was a moose lying on the tracks, napping, when the train he was on stopped and blew the whistle to make the moose move, and finally after no response, the engineer eased the train up to the moose and nudged it with the "cow catcher" and it finally got up and stepped to the side. But by that time it was so mad that it tried to bite each window as the train slowly went by. Clyde said it was a funny sight, that big head, swinging from side to side and the open mouth and teeth hitting the glass.

It was then that Clyde took Yukon to town for the two old ladies, and the following weekend he took Johnnie. We did miss the dogs, they had become great pets, but there was still Copper, and he got all the love lavished on him alone for quite some time.

Clyde said to expect some bunk beds and doors on the next freight. He bought the bunk beds at the base surplus store, and the unfinished doors were on sale. We needed them for the extra room, one door would be from the kitchen to the room, and the outer door, which was solid, would be from the room to the outside, at the front of the house. So we then would have a front door as well as a back door, at last. And the bunks were for all the extra company we were expecting, or at least hoping for, when summer came. We were making a bedroom for Clyde and I out of the room addition we had been using for storage and wood, or hanging meat in. The bunks would fit nicely where our bed was, and also where Shelley's bed was and her bed would be moved into the kitchen where the old heavy couch was. It got destroyed by a bucket of paint Clyde accidentally tipped over on it when we were painting and had to be hauled out and eventually burned.

Early in April we went into Anchorage, all of us, and had our check ups done. Everyone was in great shape, except the doctor insisted I have my gall bladder ex-rayed. When that was done he told me I should have it out at once, since the dye they put in me didn't even get to the gall bladder. It was packed with stones, he said, and then proceeded to lecture me on neglect, and that with four children I should take better care of myself. He said that living where I did I could die if I had an attack and the duct burst. He said there would be no time to get me to a hospital, etc. In other words, he scared me half to death. So I went home, packed enough clothes for myself and the kids and came back. The doctor told me to expect to stay in the hospital for ten days to two weeks, that it was major surgery, dangerous, and to be prepared. Also that I would have to stay in town at least that long, or longer while recuperating.

April 14th the surgery was performed, and when I came to, I was attached to two different machines, and an intravenous feeding pole. One tube in my nose, clear down to my stomach, two tubes coming out of the front of my stomach, next to the incision, one to drain blood attached to a suction machine, and one to drain bile from the duct to a bag attached to my leg, for the 'excess gall' with nowhere to go. It took three nurses to get me out of bed the next day and take three steps to a chair. One to hold on to me, and one for each of the two machines and the feeding pole attached to me. I was so weak I thought I'd never recover! I felt like something out of a monster movie and Clyde didn't want to bring the kids to see me because he thought it would scare them to see all that stuff attached to me.

At any rate I did recover, and healed much faster than the doctor ever thought I would. He said it was more serious than he expected because there were stones trapped in the duct as well, which he had to excise. But I managed to get out of the hospital in just 8 days and go to the little trailer where Clyde and our poor bored kids were staying. It was so crowded and uncomfortable that I begged the doctor to let me go home as soon as the stitches were out. He said I might, but only if I promised not to do anything at all for at least six weeks! Especially no lifting of any kind. I promised. I would do anything to get out of town.

But I must say that is a terrible way to lose weight! I was skinny as a rail and weak as a newborn and felt all bones and knobs.

We all went thankfully home, and Clyde and the kids saw to it that I did nothing. I even got a ride to the house on the sled, then went right to bed and slept. Clyde organized the kids so that they did all the chores, and Bud took care of feeding the fires and they all hauled in water so I did not have to lift a thing. There was still two and a half feet of snow, but the weather never got below 38 to 40 during the day. Early mornings the snow was hard packed and Clyde hauled up 18-foot logs for the woodshed with the snow machine, which he had shipped up the week before we got home. It was a dandy machine, and worked harder than the dogs ever could.

Buddy shot a spruce hen and a squirrel with his .410 shotgun. He had become quite a good shot, but he only used it with Clyde or me supervising. But I was unable to supervise for a while. So Bud did his shooting only on weekends while his dad was home and with him. So far he had shot a total of 30 ptarmigan since January.

I had 300 plants in peat pots all ready to plant, but there was still snow on the ground, and I had done nothing physical since coming home form the hospital, at all except walk a little. Everything simply wore me out. We were hopelessly behind in schoolwork by that time, when who should get off the train but my great Uncle Fred, (my mother's uncle) and his girl friend Carmen.

Uncle Fred was in his 70's at that time, and Carmen much younger, a retired Marine Sergeant. They flew up from California and somehow we did not get any letter or message that they were coming. The letter came later, of course. I had no idea how I would be able to entertain them, as I still slept much of the day. But I had no real need to worry, as Carmen took charge of everything immediately and ordered the kids around like the ex-Marine sergeant she used to be. She had that house scrubbed and cleaned until I didn't recognize it and the kids were worn out with all the work she had them do. All the walls had the coal smoke scrubbed off and the floors, well; they had never been so clean since the house was built! All I had to do was stagger out of bed or easy chair, and cook meals. Everything I cooked was the least labor intensive, but no one seemed to mind at all.

Great Uncle Fred was enjoying himself tremendously, exploring with the gun, of course, and the kids loved showing him around. At least when they were doing that, they didn't have to work as hard. Uncle Fred was a great fishing enthusiast, and enjoyed trying to catch a trout from the creek though it was still a bit early for that. There was a huge iceberg blocking the mouth of the creek. The snow was almost gone, but still nippy at night, even though it didn't get totally dark.

Carmen was certainly a workhorse, and never seemed to stop. I was grateful for the help. When able, I walked up or down the tracks with Uncle Fred and the kids in the nice sunny weather.

It was close to the end of May and Clyde's mom was arriving about June 1st. She decided to spend another summer with us; she liked it here so much. Uncle Fred and Carmen were leaving, taking the train to Anchorage on May 28th, and flying back to California about the 31st. We enjoyed Uncle Fred, the kids did not enjoy Carmen at all, but I did. We all went in on the 28th, because I had an appointment to see the doctor on the 29th. Uncle Fred said he would be back later on when the salmon were running. By the time we took the train in, I was feeling much better, more like my old self, but still sort of weak. The doctor was amazed and gave me a clean bill of health with a warning not to lift heavy stuff yet. "Give it a chance", he said.

Clyde came home on Friday, the 16th of June, and we all, including Mom rode the train up to Chulitna, got off and walked a mile back through the woods to a homestead of a friend who worked on the base with Clyde. Then we came back on the southbound train. It was a lovely hot day- too hot, really. It was more like a California heat wave, actually. We had our five plus acres of garden all in and up and growing, but were having to water it all since it had been so hot and dry.

The next day was our twelfth wedding anniversary and both our birthdays. I was 31! Clyde was 39. Some men came up the path with a lovely big rainbow trout they had caught in the mouth of our creek and gave it to us. They were part of a crew parked on the siding just south. So we knew fishing season was on once again.

Then the weather became chilly and damp and it rained and poured and once again the plants stopped growing and sat there in puddles of water like the last time Mom Lovel was here. At least we did have a week or so of hot dry weather at the beginning of Mom's visit that time. We had to keep a fire going in the barrel stove to keep the damp and chill out of the house. It was the end of June, and we were working hard at school trying to get it done, since we had gotten so far behind. We finished about mid-July. At least we didn't have to feel guilty about the weeds in the garden since it was too muddy to wade in and pull them.

Eventually the rains cleared somewhat, and the garden did grow, but it was nothing like as good as the summer before. Mom Lovel worked out in the garden every chance she got. I was grateful.

Chapter 18   Family Visits

U nfortunately, it began raining harder about the time my parents came in August. It had taken them much longer to drive up the Alcan than they had thought, even though they did not have any engine trouble or tire trouble. They did have to stop often so Grandma could get out and walk around a bit. She was quite elderly, nearing 80 years old, and got stiff from sitting so long in one position. It rained all the way up the Alcan, and they saw no wild animals at all, the whole trip, which was a huge disappointment.

Since it took them so long, they only had about four or five days to stay here since my Mom was a school teacher and had to be back in California in time for the opening day of school. But Dad loved the country and hunted every day but saw nothing. Grandma and Mom Lovel became fast friends, and Grandma loved it here as well. She went out in the rain and picked berries and worked in the garden regardless of the weather. Grandma pointed out that there were four generations of oldest daughters there in my house.

My grandma was the oldest of her mom's family; my mom was the oldest of Grandma's family; I was the oldest of my mom's family, and Shelley was the oldest of my family. Mom Lovel took a picture of the four of us, she said, for posterity.

Four generations of eldest daughters
Rachel Jaques & her daughter Rachel Zirwes & her
daughter Mary Lovel & her daughter Shelley Lovel

My two youngest brothers, Bob and Paul wanted to stay so badly that after talking it over with Mom and Dad, they agreed thinking that Bob and Paul were big enough to help me quite a bit. Bob was 15 and a big husky strong guy, almost six foot two and Paul was 11 and strong for his age, as well. Paul was still growing, but was close to my height of five foot eight at that time. Mom and Dad thought it might be a good adventure for the boys and so when it was time to leave, we all went along, except Mom Lovel. She opted to stay and feed and water Copper, and just catch up on answering mail.

Dad and Mom decided to leave the travel trailer they hauled up with them for us to sell, because they thought it would be easier to drive back without it. When we got to Talkeetna, there was no gas in the tank of Dad's car and Clyde discovered, after putting gas from a five gallon can in it that the gas tank was full of holes, most likely from the rocks on the Talkeetna Spur Road, since it had held gas all up the Alcan with no leaks. It seemed the rubber pad Dad had installed to keep rocks from hitting the tank had slipped and was actually deflecting rocks to the tank. So we had to wait for a tank for the car for a few hours, and then went on our way. In Anchorage Mom and Dad shopped for winter things for the boys. It would certainly be a big change for them.

We hated to see them go, it had been so long since I had seen my family at all, but we understood the necessity. While we were in Anchorage for those two days, Great Uncle Fred came back, and he went home with us on the train the next day. He was delighted to meet

Clyde's mom and also that the fish were in, and he spent many hours catching salmon until we begged him to stop. We were tired of eating fish and so I canned up whatever he caught for the rest of his stay, and sent much of it home with him.

Bob caught fish and Buddy also and finally Paul and all the kids wrote to Mom and Dad and Grandma. Paul's first letter to them since they left went like this:

"Dear Mom, Dad and all,

We are building a woodshed and Shelley got mad at me because Bud was making me laugh. The fish are spawning now and I never get a chance to use the net because Bobby is using it all the time, but Mary said I get it tomorrow. Yesterday Buddy and me saw a bear and today we almost got hit by a train while we were on the railroad bridge over the creek. We ran. It is sunny and hot now.

Love, Paul - PS: I caught three fish."

That letter must have given Mom and Dad some serious doubts as well as a scare or two, at least some misgivings. I too wrote them, only in more detail. Especially about getting caught on the bridge by a train. I was with the boys and it was the most frightening thing. The three boys and I took the wheelbarrow across the bridge and picked up broken pieces of railroad ties that were soaked with creosote, for kindling. The usual number of trains had already gone by and we thought we were safe to cross that bridge. We were in the middle, halfway back over the bridge toward home with the loaded wheel barrow, and of course couldn't hear anything because of the water rushing by in the creek, but when I looked up and saw that big monster train engine bearing down on us just at the same time the engineer honked and put on the brakes, well, that was the most terrifying thing! Buddy jumped over the side and hung on, and Bobby and Paul ran back to the other end of the bridge. I threw the wheelbarrow over the side and ran also. We just barely made it and the train went on past. But it was way too close for comfort!

Shortly after that, since the fishing had slowed down to a trout now and then, Great Uncle Fred left us to return to California, and took his two cases of canned salmon with him. He had finished building the woodshed with Bobby's help and mine.

Then a few days later, Clyde's mom left as well. I think the noise level in our cabin was too much for her by that time.

Mom ordered school materials for the boys, and Paul's came toward the end of September, but Bobby's didn't come until about the end of October. So he had to really dig in to catch up. He was in tenth grade, and Paul was in 7th grade, same as Shelley. Paul was seven months younger than his niece, by the way. Much of our time was spent digging and sacking potatoes.

We got a front quarter of moose from the crew on the Sherman siding in trade for fresh vegetables and 100 pounds of potatoes. We were happy to get the fresh meat. We had the cellar full of potatoes, and 20 to 30 sacks in each bedroom besides. But Clyde eventually got them all sold, except for the ones in the cellar. Each weekend when he came home he brought several hundred pounds of potatoes back to town with him until there were no more sacks in the bedrooms.

September 3rd was Bobby's birthday, he was 16. Paul would be 12 on October 21st.

Around the end of September we had a fantastic display of northern lights dancing all over the sky. The next night the temperature was down to freezing. The boys were such a big help to me - while I was supervising the other kids' school, Bob and Paul were out hauling wood from the wood piles with the tractor, also keeping the water barrels filled from the creek.

October 16th we witnessed the full eclipse of the moon. It was 15 degrees that night, but usually was 35 to 40 during the day. Each and every night it was colder than the night before. We had three inches of snow on the ground but we were still hauling wood with the tractor. Bob split and the boys packed and stacked, and we all helped haul sometimes. Usually the girls and I stayed home and cleaned house and cooked, but occasionally we went out to help too.

Paul was getting along fine with his school courses; he said the modern math was easy for him, since he was used to it, and had it for several years by then.

About two weeks before I heard a noise outside under the porch and when I looked to see what it was, there was a gray cat with white markings around the collar and chest area, tummy and feet. He was very pretty and seemed well mannered and turned out to be a great mouser. I had no idea where he came from. The kids all liked him and named him 'Hoiman' – (that was Bobby's idea) and the name stuck. He was housebroken too, which was a plus. But most of the time he preferred to stay outside, and caught at least 4 or 5 mice a day that we knew of, that he didn't eat, at least. Much later we found out he was one of Nellie's cats that she couldn't find when it was time to leave for Kenai. Somehow he made it all the way down here from Gold Creek, seeking a friendly family to move in with, I guess.

Norma Jean came down on Wednesday and stayed until Saturday. She brought her rock and roll records with her and the kids all had a blast dancing to the music, and our house shook from time to time with all the racket. No schoolwork was done.

My mom sent a typewriter, (manual of course), ice skates for the boys, books and magazines and we got a whole ton of mail. Thank goodness for Leroy, the track patrolman. When he stopped at Gold Creek, he saw there were two huge bags of mail there for us, and he brought them by. The section foreman seldom remembered. Also my mom wrote that she had received no mail from us for at least a month, and was concerned. We wrote at least once a week, and I left the mail out in the box for whoever would pick it up. Finally we sent it all in to town with Clyde, because evidently it was not getting mailed at all. I wonder whatever happened to the missing mail.

It snowed day and night for two weeks from about November 7th to the 21st or so. Shelley and I went to Anchorage on the 12th and there was already three feet of snow on the ground. I had to go for a checkup and Shelley needed some dental work done. The snowplow had not been by yet and when the passenger train stopped for us we all got buried by the snow spray from the engine. We dug our way out and climbed, snow and all, on to the train. Clyde stayed home with the rest of the kids. There was no snow at all from Talkeetna clear to Anchorage. It was like stepping into a different world. The doctor said I was fine, but needed to gain 10 or 15 pounds because I was underweight! Me! I couldn't believe it. He also said I needed to relax a little more and not work so hard! Wow.

We got back home the 14th. There was nearly five feet of snow (still none in Anchorage) and was still snowing occasionally, mixed with rain. By the 22nd we had seven feet. We couldn't move anywhere without snowshoes, and had to pack and re-pack the trails to the creek and the woodpiles or the snow machine would get stuck. We couldn't get to the woodpiles, actually, so we had to cut down a few trees directly behind the house in that patch of woods, close, to tide us over until it turned cold enough that the wet gooey snow froze dry and packed down. Nearly every day we had to dig our way to the outhouse and woodshed. We couldn't find the trash dump so had to stack boxes of tin cans in the woodshed until we could dig to the dump. Copper was let loose since his doghouse was far under the snow and we knew we'd never find it until spring. The cat, Hoiman, was by then a permanent resident inside the house because he sunk out of sight if he stepped off a path, and besides he wouldn't go out since Copper was loose and the snow was so deep and very wet.

We were so busy all the time that the days just rushed by and then it was Christmas, then New Years and another year started. All the kids got along together just fine, for which I was thankful. Feeding six growing kids was a chore. I thought four were bad enough, but add two more, and wow. But I just increased my bread baking, and cinnamon roll making and cake baking and cooked huge pots of beans and stew and lots of potatoes always, and somehow we all got enough to eat. The boys really worked hard, though and needed to eat to keep up their strength.

Mom and Dad sent checks every month to supplement our income and to be sure we got fresh fruit once in a while, at least, and of course for clothes and things for the boys.

We were afraid the boys would get totally tired of it here, being used to city life and everything, but they still seemed to like it a lot, even with all the snow.

Bobby taught me how to play the guitar, some basic chords at least, and he practiced a lot on it. He had brought, and Mom had sent a bunch of music books, some Beatles tunes among others, and since Bobby and I could read music, we learned some of them. Bobby had a great singing voice too, and most of my kids and I could at least carry a tune, and Paul could sing very well too. So we had our musical evenings.

Mom sent an accordion up and a harmonica and Bobby's clarinet. We had quite a band going. I ordered a small drum set for Christmas for Clyde so he could join in on our musical evenings. It was fun. We had a great Christmas, with lots of music, and fun. But we sure missed Mom and Dad, and Grandma too.

In February I got my first shots at a moose. Buddy and Paul had been out hunting for ptarmigan with the .410 shotgun, and sighted the moose, ran home to get me, and what a total failure that was! I had completely forgotten about setting the sight distance, and it was set on 900 yards, but the moose I was shooting at was only about 100 yards away, and I emptied the 30.06 rifle, (six shots) at him and missed!!! He just looked at me with great disdain, (I thought) and calmly walked away. The snow was too crusty to walk on in snowshoes, but we followed him to where he went down to the river and across to a little island north of the house, where there was a gang of six men working on the tracks, and gave it up. That was too many witnesses! But the next day, that same moose came back across the river and pestered the men until they could get no work done, and even came up our creek path and stood gazing at the house, but we could not shoot him with that many people around. Oh, but we needed meat so badly by then!

The next morning the moose was back pestering the men and I heard a shot, looked out and just then along came a station wagon blowing the horn, and the moose went north again. Next we heard the men shouting and the gas car engine racing so we gathered the moose was still around. The next day, early, the gas car stopped out front and a man came to the door and said they had a moose out at the tracks for us that the train had hit early that morning and I thought it was the same one we shot at because he said it had come from the island and they'd had to throw flares at him all day to get rid of him the day before and that the train had hit him early that morning. So they cut off his head, and all four legs below the knees, dumped the whole un-gutted moose on the sled after having dragged it three miles behind the gas car, then all eight men dragged it on our sled to the house and left. So before we even had breakfast Bud, Paul, Shelley and I skinned and gutted it, cut it in quarters and hung it up. It was the easiest moose I'd had to skin out. Some of the meat was damaged because of all the rough treatment it got, but most of it was good, and so the happy homesteaders had abundant meat once more. Then we had breakfast.

Bobby could not help because he was sick, but as soon as he was better he would get his own moose. He was racing right along with school and ready to take finals.

By the time the snow was packed enough to run the snow machine, it wouldn't run. First the gas line broke, we fixed that, then the spark plug wire came apart, and we fixed that. The drive belt broke, and we bought a new one. But meanwhile, we ran Copper again to drag in wood. When we got the new spark plug, the snow machine ran fine for three days and then quit again. I had no idea what was wrong that time, so Copper was employed once again. It was a good thing we had him. He really didn't mind, he loved to run and pull the sled.

We thought Bobby just had a cold, because Clyde had one when he came home two weeks before, but Bobby just kept getting worse, so he went in on the train to see a doctor and the doctor made some tests and said Bobby had mononucleosis. I don't recall what the treatment was then, but he got over it in time and was back to normal once again and none of the rest of us caught it from him. Living in such a small place, I thought that was remarkable.

The first week of March Clyde had an accident with his motorcycle while on the way to work. They had told him on the base that he had to put a third wheel on his motorcycle for safety to run in the winter, otherwise he wouldn't be allowed on base, and whoever put it on, did not have it centered just right, so the first corner he turned, it flipped him over and broke his collarbone and three ribs. No other cuts, just bruises and no other serious injuries. He came home Saturday for the entire week to rest up. They told him at the hospital it would take about six weeks for his bones to mend enough for him to be very active.

We had the wonderful hard-as-concrete snow, and we made a day of it. We all went out into the woods, Bobby cut down 25 trees and Buddy and I and Paul cut them up. Clyde supervised, and built a big fire, even though it was warm and sunny, and we had a picnic and roasted marshmallows for dessert. The younger boys took turns hauling the cut wood home with the snow machine and with Copper. The girls stacked, and we got a lot done, and had fun doing it, too. Around the 19th or 20th of March (1968) the day after Clyde and Bobby went back to town, two men from the Bureau of Land Department got out of a bush plane flown by Don Sheldon, which landed on the river ice in front of our house, and came up on snowshoes to inspect our plowing (under six feet of snow). It had only taken them a year and seven months to make it. They estimated our acreage plowed, and passed us with flying colors, though how they could tell anything about plowed or planted ground under six feet of snow was beyond me! They took pictures and flew off again. Bud and Paul talked the poor pilot to death asking questions. They were sure thrilled watching the plane land and take off.

All that was left for us to do then was wait for the surveyors to come, probably in the summer, and the land department would notify us when to advertise our claim in the paper for five weeks, and possibly then we would get title to the land.

Bobby had gone in to help Clyde out and for his final exams for school and to have a last check-up with the doctor. They came back the following weekend. Bobby was fine, and Clyde was still sore but they put him to work at a desk type job for a while. With his cracked ribs and broken collarbone, finally the railroad called him to go to work at Gold Creek. But he had to pass the physical first. The railroad doctor asked him how high he could raise his arms and Clyde could only raise them up waist high, but the doctor passed him anyway. He had two weeks to go on the base and started working for the railroad April 22nd. Meanwhile, Bobby hurt his knee and couldn't walk and we got help, two guys carried him out on a stretcher and put him on the train to town where an ambulance met him and took him to the hospital. Clyde met him there, and after x-rays the doctor found a bone chip cutting into the cartilage and said he'd have to operate. Clyde called Mom and Dad in California to let them know and arrangements were made. Meanwhile, while Bobby was being operated on and under anesthesia, Clyde got word that his brother Wayne was just killed in an auto accident in California and Mom Lovel begged him to come and help settle things for Pat, his wife. They had seven children. Clyde hurriedly called and left word for me to pack up the kids and get to town to be with Bobby and he caught a plane and left for California.

Kids and I packed up and left the next day and stayed with friends in town, while Bobby was recovering in the hospital. The patrolman fed Copper while we were gone, and everything was fine here, but poor Clyde was devastated by the loss of his brother, who was only two years older than Clyde. They were very close. He managed to get things settled for Pat, and after the funeral he came back, put in the rest of his time on the base and packed up and we all went home to Sherman. Two days later, Clyde went to work for the railroad at Gold Creek. There were quarters there where he could sleep if necessary, and sometimes he got a ride home with one of the passing gas cars, or his boss. But usually he had to walk the five miles to work in the mornings. Most nights he was home and we actually felt like a family again. I had been ready to give it all up after two and a half years of part time family life.

Two weeks after Clyde started working for the Railroad we finally got our telephone installed. We had our name on the list for more than two years but the railroad insisted we have a phone, and we paid for the wire to be run and then we had one. It was a 10 party line.

Clyde and Bob both healed well, and by June when our Mom came, Bob and Paul and I went to town to meet her plane. It was so good to have her here, and we wished Dad had come as well. But he wasn't feeling very well, and he wouldn't fly, for any reason. So he stayed back in California with Grandma. Mom had really missed the boys so much, but they didn't want to leave yet, and so Mom told them they could stay on awhile if it was okay with us. Of course it was!

That summer was hot and sunny and we had to water the potatoes most of the summer, and what a job that was! The little water pump and lots of garden hose helped out quite a bit. All the vegetables thrived and the manager of the McKinley Park Hotel, once he heard about our lush gardens, arranged with the conductors of the passenger trains to have us send boxes of produce to him, since he wasn't having much luck getting fresh vegetables for the hotel dining room. He sent us a letter by train asking us to send whatever produce was ready, and he would send money back by the next train. And so we did. We packed big beautiful cauliflower, broccoli, cabbages, leaf lettuce, green onions, radishes, beets turnips, and carrots. Also rhubarb. Lots and lots of it. He wanted a box a week, at least, he said, and he was faithful about sending a check back for whatever he thought the produce was worth. He was generous. We had lots. And when the potatoes were ready to dig, he got many of those, as well. They were big and beautiful, many of them baking size.

Mary & Lisa after the summer harvest & all the canning was done!

The surveyors had come and gone, and we had advertised for the five-weeks required, and finally, finally got our patent deed to our land, about six months later. It only took about three years from the filing of our final proof, but after that we were not obliged to do anything more. We could even sell it if we wanted to. But it was really and truly ours, at last. We were so happy.

September of 1968, all the kids and I went up in the hills behind the house and cut down some spruce trees to build a little hunting cabin and surprise Clyde with it. It was at the halfway point between the cabin and the top of the mountain. Every day when Clyde was at work, and after chores were done, we went up there, with chain saw and gas and spent several hours just cutting and hauling until we had enough to start building. When the weather was fine, and it mostly was, we put it together. But we were stumped as to how to put the roof on. Or even how to build a roof. We finally had to get Clyde up there and show him what we had been doing (instead of cutting firewood) and he certainly was surprised. Didn't take long to get the roof on then, and we had a neat little cabin in which we eventually installed a small stove, and bunks built to the wall.

School started once again, and winter came and we got no moose for quite awhile. But when we did, we got them all at once. We gladly shared with any of our neighbors who needed the meat.

Building the cabin on the bench   **More of us at the cabin**

Summer 1967 lots of company

The boys ran the trap line they set up almost every day. They caught a marten and several mink and ermine. The track patrolman at Curry stopped by and showed the boys the proper way to skin out a fur in order to sell it.

Chapter 19 Outhouse News

An outhouse is a necessary evil, especially if you have no indoor plumbing. When the outhouse was built, by the Rudders, it was only meant to be for two people's use, one of whom was absent from home more than half the time, working. Now, when all of a sudden the population rose to six people, and then to eight, something astounding happened. This little one hole outhouse filled up!!

It was April, lots of snow still on the ground, and we had company for the weekend. Doug and Marie Dunn, our friends from Anchorage and their two little girls, Julia and Beverly came and got off the train on a Saturday, so that put the population of Sherman up to twelve people. Very soon, the frozen contents of said outhouse began to rise in an inverted cone above the seat level, making it impossible to use.

Clyde, being the enterprising fellow that he is, decided to remedy the situation, and proceeded to break off chunks of said frozen material with a crow bar until it was below seat level. But he could readily see that it would not be enough, even so. He poked holes all around and put some left over dynamite caps in said holes. All the while, Doug was standing by, watching to see what would happen. Clyde put a board over the hole, weighted it down with a large rock, and lit the fuse to the dynamite caps.

When it blew up, the board and rock went onto the floor and it really went up, all over the ceiling and walls, and froze there, since it was fairly cold and well below freezing at that time. Until we got that all swept off the ceiling and walls, we could not use it at all, for fear of some of it falling onto us. Ugh!

Doug thought it was so funny he just rolled over on the snow laughing, until someone had to help him up. When they got on the train later that day to go back to Anchorage, Doug was still laughing, and told all the trainmen what happened. I guess that story circulated quite a bit, because even now, thirty five years or more later, an occasional trainman will approach one of us wanting to know if we were the ones that blew up our outhouse, and why. Talk about your embarrassing moments of life!!

Chapter 20 Family Reunion

My brothers left on March 11th, 1969 because our Dad was ill and Mom was afraid he might not make it that time. We certainly missed them both. But in April, my oldest brother, John, sent me an airline ticket to fly to California for a surprise family reunion for Mom and Dad. He had rallied some once the boys were home and was better. I think he missed them more than he thought. John also sent a ticket to my sister Beth, so we would all be there at once. Our sister Kathy was already there, and she was the only one who knew we were all coming. All she had to do was make sure Mom and Dad were home. I was gone for a week, and Clyde took that week off work to stay home with the kids, so that I could go. That was my first ever jet ride. John felt we should all go because our Dad had been having some awfully bad spells of cardiac asthma that was scaring everyone.

The flight was great, and even though I missed my connection in Los Angeles for San Diego, that airline put me on another airline so I could make it in time, and when I got across the airport, there was my sister Beth, waiting in line to board the plane I was going to take too. She was sure surprised, and we even got to sit together and ride to San Diego. Oh it was good to see her again. Of course John was worried sick when I wasn't on my plane, but so relieved when I got off Beth's plane with her. Wow, but I had missed those guys.

We really surprised Mom when we got there. She cried, she was so happy and Dad wasn't home, but we surprised him when he came in awhile later, and he almost cried. It was a very emotional time for all of us. We had a wonderful time together, and Mom said that Dad felt better than he'd felt all year and took less oxygen for his asthma all that week. It was the first time in 10 years we had all been together.

But I missed my kids and husband so much I was glad to get home. When I walked in the front door there was a great big sign, painted by the kids, and hung all across the bedroom. "Welcome home, mom, we missed you.

Back to the old routine, except I was kept busy peeling spruce logs Clyde had cut while I was gone. He'd decided he needed an equipment shed to house the tractor, snow machine, and the new Ranger track vehicle we bought earlier that year.

Clyde didn't have to take off work while I was gone after all. There was a relief foreman, a very nice man, and a pleasure to work for, Clyde said. He dropped Clyde off after work, and picked him up in the mornings, and let him off at home at noon so he could have lunch with the kids and see that everything was all right. He even managed to be working in the vicinity of the house the entire week. I thought that was wonderful. And Shelley was, after all, 14 by then and very responsible.

The kids always knew just where they would be working so it was really wonderful and Clyde didn't have to use up any of his vacation time, which he wanted to save to take off for building the roof and hunting fishing and gardening at each appropriate time. We planned to put a peak roof on the house that spring, which would add more living space as well.

The snow was all gone but the ground still frozen. We planned to have a big garden again that year, even though we did not have to. But we felt it was a waste not to; after all, things did grow well and it really saved a bundle on our grocery bill. The bears were all out, and one day in late May Clyde came home from work feeling awful with a head cold, and stayed home for the next two days. It was a sunny hot day, I was cooking lunch and Clyde was soaking up the sun talking to Bud about areas to be plowed in the garden and where we would be putting what crops that year, when Debbie came running through the house yelling, "Mom, Mom, there's a big black bear out back and he looked at me!!!" So I ran out to see, and sure enough, there was a beautiful shiny black bear rather large, standing at the edge of the dump placidly looking us over. Our great watchdogs were asleep. (By that time we had acquired a pretty female (Lassie) half collie and half husky). I ran back in and made sure all the kids were inside and yelled for Clyde. He came in the front and grabbed the gun and Bud grabbed the shells and got target ammunition by mistake, (which were not as powerful as regular shells) and Clyde took off out the back door with Bud right behind him with the other rifle. The bear wasn't in sight, so the first thing we thought was that he took off. After walking a few feet, Clyde discovered he was down in the ditch, tossing the tin cans around and just then Bud yelled, "There he is, Dad!" When the bear raised his head up Clyde shot him in the eye. Because it was a target shell, it came out the back of his head. He flopped a few times and then got up and ran back into the woods. Clyde shot him again in the neck as he ran and they loaded both rifles with the right ammunition and took off after the bear, and found it across the creek. It had run a good half-mile and was sitting in a hollow between two cottonwood trees licking the blood off its front leg where it had run out of his neck. Bud shot him again, finally killing him.

They came back home and got the Ranger, drove it across the creek and up to the edge of the woods and piled the whole bear, (about 350 pounds of it) on the metal-bottomed sled and dragged it home. I canned the whole bear all day Saturday while Bud and Clyde planted potatoes. Got 38 quarts canned and cooked all the fat and bones and scraps for the dogs. Sunday we finished planting potatoes and all week we planted everything else including cabbages etc. We picked our first batch of rhubarb on the last day of May.

Our old generator burnt out a valve, and the garden tiller had a burnt clutch. We had to wait for parts for both machines before we could fix them.

Lassie was due to have puppies in about a month, and Copper had quills in his face from biting a porcupine.

The kids were all done with school except for Shelley, she had a week or so left.

Mom Lovel came again for the summer and we were expecting Clyde's sister Lou and her husband Fred and their four children, John, Jim, Joan and Julie whenever they arrived. They were driving up some time in July from Missouri.

Building the upstairs on the house at Sherman, Alaska

Soon the lumber Clyde had ordered arrived, and over the 4th of July weekend he built the peak roof on the house. He bought a portable staircase, I guess it was called, one that could be folded up to the ceiling and fastened. But he fixed it so it would not fold up and it was fastened securely to the floor from the hole in the ceiling next to the inside wall separating the kitchen from the bedroom, which rapidly became our living room. The kids all got the upstairs, which was one big room, divided by the stairway. The largest side of the room was for the three girls, and the smallest side was Buddy's.

We decided that the house needed to be painted on the outside. The original two rooms were a sort of faded green color, mostly peeling, and of course the upstairs of all new lumber, wasn't painted at all.

When we went to town for the paint we bought two five-gallon cans of white paint, and two tubes of thalo green color (one for each five gallon can) to mix in to make it green paint. That is what was recommended by the man at the paint store. When we got it home and mixed it up, it turned turquoise blue, which was sort of green, but much prettier than the green that was already on the house. Clyde painted every chance he got, and was nearly finished with the first coat of paint when the train stopped and Fred and Lou and kids all got off. Wow, we had a house full once again. They stayed for six weeks. But meanwhile my mom wrote that she and my sister Beth were coming in early August, and she enclosed an article from the El Cajon Valley newspaper, which said, "Rachel Zirwes and her daughter Beth Zirwes will be visiting Rachel's oldest daughter, Mary Lovel, where she lives in the City of Sherman, Alaska."

Fred thought that was a real hoot, because of where we lived, there was absolutely nothing or no one for miles and miles in either direction! Our "City" was populated by six people, two dogs, one cat and other transient populations from time-to-time. "Some city," said Fred.

While Clyde and I went to Anchorage to meet my mom and my sister Beth at the airport, Fred wanted something to do, so Clyde told him he could finish painting the house, if he wanted to. And that was what Fred did. When we got off the train with my mom and Beth, there was this big shining turquoise blue house with a large sign on the upstairs stating, "SHERMAN CITY HALL", Wow. The tourists all thought that was so funny, and took pictures and my mom and Beth also thought that it was certainly different. We all got a laugh out of it. And the train men, over the years, have all told us to never paint the sign out, because it was such a big hit with the tourists, and something to talk about. So we have kept it touched up every time we have to paint the house, and the sign is basically the same as it was when Fred painted it.

We still live here, and have our various adventures from time to time. Life is never dull or boring. We still have company every summer from the States, and sometimes friends from Anchorage come up and of course our children and their wonderful spouses, and 13 grandchildren as well. We have never built a new cabin, just fixed this old one up from time-to-time, when boards needed replacing or the floor or the roof. It suits us. We keep thinking, 'maybe some day'.

We have better machines now, of course, and they break down from time-to-time as well. We travel sometimes when the mood strikes and we have the money saved up.

My mom and dad are both gone now, and also my beloved sister, Beth. We miss them so much. Clyde's mom spent many summers with us, but we lost her in 2004 at ninety-nine years, seven months. She was last here when she was 92.

Brother Bobby has made his life work music, and is very successful with a large recording studio, many CD's and a large following of fans along with his business partner and best friend, also named Bob.

Paul has a successful business building computer systems and programming them, and in partnership with brother John who sells the systems Paul builds.

Our life is a simple one and tranquil for the most part, and we hope to be able to stay here in Sherman City Hall for many more years. God willing.

The journey was long and hard, but our dream has been fulfilled beyond our wildest expectations.

Sherman City Hall - Sherman, Alaska - The end of the rainbow

THE END

Glossary

- **adze** — A Hoe-like axe used to chop roots out of the ground

- **bench** — The flattening of a hillside partway up a mountain

- **bush** — Way out in the country, usually with no road access available

- **Cheechako** — A newcomer or greenhorn

- **Chinook** — A warm wind typically blowing from the south

- **Outside** — Anywhere NOT in Alaska; also "lower 48" or stateside

- **Scythe** — An old fashioned long curved blade with a long handle for cutting grass, brush and weeds

- **Slough** — (pronounced slew) a small portion of a river; an area where it becomes a pond or slow-moving stream eventually re-joining the river.

- **STATES** — 48 contiguous states separated from Alaska by Canada

Made in the USA
Columbia, SC
26 October 2023

24963112R00105